2 Tim. 1:7

Mandy Belmont ☺

"*Mind What Matters* tackles a topic most people just brush off. What does it mean to have a 'sound mind'? Is it just a phrase uttered in the reading of a will? How can we 'take every thought captive' and in so doing develop a sound mind? Amanda Belmont's new book represents more than a personal journey. It represents a careful and accurate study of the mind from God's perspective. I highly recommend it!"

—**BILL HENNESSY**, executive director of operations, Life360 Community Services

"In this insightful book, Amanda Belmont engages her reader with her easy writing style and her in-depth research into the human mind. This is a theologically sound book with biblical insights and references that help the reader understand the power of the human mind and how every person has the ability to change their thinking when they align it with biblical principles. Every pastor, youth leader, and ministry student should read this book. I highly recommend it."

—**CAROL ALEXANDER**, dean of the Graduate School, Trinity Bible College and Graduate School

"Drawing upon both the wisdom of the early church *and* contemporary clinical psychology, Amanda Belmont unpacks what it means for us to have a truly sound mind. Then, she lays out research-based suggestions for achieving it. This book is both well-researched and well-written, a punchy must-read for anyone interested in the topic."

—**MATTHEW PAYNE**, vice president of student services, Trinity Bible College & Graduate School

"Our thoughts matter, and learning to focus them on the right things is of the utmost importance. Amanda Belmont does a wonderful job laying a solid biblical framework from which to approach developing a sound mind. She also gives practical steps that the reader can take to develop a mind that seeks to love and honor God. I highly recommend this book."

—KEVIN LIBBY, lead pastor, New Life Assembly of God

Mind What Matters

Mind What Matters

A Theology of Developing a Sound Mind

Amanda Belmont

Forewords by
Scott Townsend
and *Noel Sanderson*

WIPF & STOCK · Eugene, Oregon

MIND WHAT MATTERS
A Theology of Developing a Sound Mind

Wipf & Stock
An Imprint of Wipf and Stock Publishers
199 W. 8th Ave., Suite 3
Eugene, OR 97401

www.wipfandstock.com

PAPERBACK ISBN: 978-1-6667-6010-1
HARDCOVER ISBN: 978-1-6667-6011-8
EBOOK ISBN: 978-1-6667-6012-5

02/14/23

This book is dedicated to all the men and
women of God who seek to love him more,
starting with the thoughts in their minds.

For God has not given us a spirit of fear, but of
power and of love and of a sound mind.

—2 TIMOTHY 1:7 (NKJV)

Contents

Foreword

I HAVE HAD THE distinguished honor to supervise Amanda in her master's thesis. Once I heard the title, *Mind What Matters*, I knew I wanted to be a part of this project. The journey from beginning, to development, to conclusion was an exciting opportunity for me to read her discoveries on developing a sound mind in the midst of all the distractions that vie for our attention.

Amanda, or Mandy, as she's known to us, has a fun, celebratory, and personally driven personality. From the time she walked on this campus as an undergraduate student, to the time that we were able to sign off on her thesis, she has exemplified the marks of mindfulness from a distinctly Christian perspective.

In spite of being a believer myself, I have had challenging moments of inner confusion, lack of focus and direction. Having worked through many of those challenges with the help of Scripture and other resources, I was excited to work with Mandy as part of my own journey to mental and spiritual health. Often, we would find ourselves in discussion of some point or direction she wanted to develop in her thesis. These discussions were as much if not even more beneficial for me as I was encouraged and helped by the information we discussed.

Soon after her graduation, Mandy asked about publishing her thesis. After some prayer and research, she landed on a publisher and granted me an opportunity to write part of the forward for her book. I am honored to be part of not only Mandy's journey, but further discovery as an author and researcher on such an important topic.

Mandy's thesis, on the surface, shares commonalities with self-help books. The issue, however, is that self-help books abound. As I typed "self-help books" into my Amazon search field, the results say ". . . over seventy thousand results for 'self help books'" What's more, is when I type 'self help books' into a Google search field, over 3.8 billion results come up. Among these books, the topics range from "abuse," "anger management," "eating disorders," "healthy relationships," and many more. Do we really need one more? Will another self-help book simply become white noise?

Amanda's book, *Mind What Matters*, approaches personal development from a different perspective than self-help. Her book begins with the chapter, "It all starts with a thought." Thoughts are personal things. They are mine. No one else in the world knows what I am thinking. That is a good thing. If my thoughts were opened for everyone to see, all kinds of good and bad could come from that. Just as they are personal, they also influence me in several ways.

Good thoughts can have wonderfully transformative and powerful influences on my heart and mind both physically and spiritually. However, bad thoughts can have destructive consequences. In Matthew 5:28, Jesus said, "But I tell you that anyone who looks at a woman lustfully has already committed adultery in his heart." My thoughts have deceived me. Although I may not act on this thought, I have allowed this thought to take root in such a way that my relationships could very well be compromised.

Jesus didn't leave us waffling when he warned us of lustful thoughts. In response, he said, in Matthew 5:29, "If your right eye causes you to stumble, gouge it out and throw it away." Thankfully, Jesus didn't intend for his listeners, or readers, to follow his advice verbatim. Rather, take drastic measures when thoughts move us in ways that don't honor those around us. Basically, Jesus means that we should be people who discipline ourselves, not only in what we look at, but what we think.

Mandy's purpose behind writing her book was "to develop a theology of a sound mind." Insightfully, Mandy notes that, "Thoughts are essential, and the things one allows one's mind to think about matters. Developing a sound mind takes intentionality and discipline." Intentionality is an important and oft overlooked concept in our part of the world. Too often, it seems like we react to things that happen to us rather than intentionally discipline ourselves to direct our hearts and minds in association with things that happen around us. Intentionality is the discipline of making up one's mind to respond to life in a disciplined manner. Mandy's book addresses the importance of intentionality in a variety of areas of life.

The chapters that Mandy has put forward challenges the reader to be intentionally disciplined in the areas of focus, meditation, diet and exercise, and rest and relaxation. Each of these components of life are addressed from the perspective of scripture and other godly authors that have spoken into those subjects. So, the question I asked earlier, I ask again. Do we really need another self-help book?

No. But I don't consider this a self-help book. Rather a book about intentionality and self-discipline with the help of God's Word and the Holy Spirit in our lives. Paul the apostle said in response to the Corinthians who had concerns about eating food sacrificed to idols, in 1 Corinthians 10:23–24, "'I have the right to do anything,' you say—but not everything is beneficial. 'I have the right to do anything'—but not everything is constructive. No one should seek their own good, but the good of others." Paul here reminds his readers, including us, that whatever we do, we do in honor of the Lord and of others.

Mandy, in her book, has done the same. She reminds her readers that with appropriate constraint, life is lived to its fullest. As a wage earner, If I were to spend every cent I make on things that I want right now, I would have nothing left for the things I need like my mortgage, food, car payment, lights, and so on. I must constrain myself to live a fuller life. The areas of life that Mandy addresses in her book remind us that with constraint and discipline, we can live life to the fullest as we submit ourselves to the Lord, love him, and live as members of his kingdom today. I pray that you are as encouraged and challenged by the insights that Mandy shares as I have been.

Scott Townsend, PhD
Author, *Jesus' Table Talk*

Foreword

As one of her graduate school professors, I came to know Amanda (Mandy) Belmont as a serious but fun-loving student of life. Her commitment to her academic work was always impressive, especially in her thesis, out of which this book has emerged. She could have left her thesis on a shelf but determined to share what she had discovered with a wider audience. The Christian life is to be fully lived, and to do so certainly requires a sound mind. Her achievements in her research and in writing this book are commendable, and I pray, will be eminently helpful.

Amanda Belmont has undertaken a serious task in offering her readers theological and practical insights into a Christian's mind and thought life. Grounded in her own graduate research, she has offered her readers powerful and practical steps towards a Christ honoring lifestyle, especially when an individual chooses to live a life that has healthy mental, emotional, and scriptural boundaries. Not just boundaries, but sustained action steps that if mastered, can produce a sound mind. Her reaching for a theology of a sound mind may appear ambitious, but in Belmont's case, she has set out a pathway that not only makes attaining a sound mind possible but makes it accessible for her readers. This is neither a technical manual nor a self-help book, but it does contain elements of both. It is practical, Scripture-based and consequently, helpful.

Reflecting on over forty years of pastoring, it would have been helpful if the Christian circles I moved in had even an inkling of what Belmont has tackled in this book. Despite evidence that mental wellbeing was a conversation at least as far back as the Greek philosophers, so Belmont reminds us, it has in my experience, eluded too many in the church. Some may have argued that all Christians needed was more faith. Belmont differs, holding out a lamp that illuminates a path to a practical theology that can be life transforming.

For too long, mental health was either taken for granted, or left to the professionals in psychology and psychiatry. From my experience, both were viewed with suspicion and disdain. Scripture and theology addressed the needs of the soul, not the mind. Thankfully, this has changed. This book has been written in a time when mental health has become a commonly used phrase. In some instances, even misused to explain and justify human dysfunction and bad (sinful) choices. This is not a book about therapy, psychology, or any of its related fields of professional practice. Instead, Belmont has offered her readers something grounded in eternal truth, which has the power to build a healthy, sound mind. She has reminded me of some of the most basic (obvious) practices that provide the building blocks that make for a sound mind.

Each chapter is a beautiful tapestry into which she has woven Scripture, practical insights from literature, and practical steps anyone can take. Together, these create a framework that is immediately useful if one wants to develop healthy mental habits. Belmont promotes a comprehensive approach in which not one, but several practices can be effective if mental well-being is to be achieved. The reader may be pleasantly surprised at how common-sense bleeds through each chapter. From beginning to the end, the reader is introduced to a host of voices and perspectives, each one adding depth and wisdom to every chapter.

We are reminded in this work, that a sound mind is not accidently stumbled upon. Intentionality is a key to unlocking a biblically sound mind. Quoting Craig Groeschel, "You cannot change what you do not confront . . . ," Belmont reminds her readers that change starts with the courage to act. What we focus on, what we expose our minds to, what we do to rest, how we treat our bodies, all these contribute to well-developed mental health. There is indeed a battle for our minds, and I believe that this book will be useful in setting the ground work for a lasting victory for those who aspire to have the mind of Christ in everyday living. She has helped us look behind the verbiage and see the hope that a sound mind offers. In a frenetic world, the choice to stand still, be silent and listen to God can be a great healer of the mind. Her work offers more than the ethereal, she has brought the theology down to a series of practical everyday action steps, steps we can all take. It is with enthusiasm that I recommend this book to the reader.

Noel Sanderson
Trinity Graduate School
Associate Dean (Web programs)
North Dakota

Acknowledgments

WRITING A BOOK IS no small feat, and I would not be here without the help, encouragement, and inspiration of so many. My family, especially Mom and Dad, who have never swayed in their belief that I could do this. My graduate school professors, who taught, challenged, inspired, and encouraged me every step along the way. And the many amazing friends who have heard me talk endlessly about developing a theology of a sound mind. Proverbs 27:17 says, "As iron sharpens iron, so one person sharpens another." And I can honestly say, each of the people mentioned above has helped to sharpen me and better prepare me for the future.

Introduction

It All Starts with a Thought

"THERE IT WAS AGAIN, another has fallen," I thought to myself as I was scrolling through social media and saw another post from an acquaintance or friend who was posting about a life choice that was not God-honoring. Sometimes the posts were prideful, as the person boasted about the life they were now choosing to live, and sometimes they were given in an explanatory mode, where the person felt the need to expound upon where they were now, often justifying the decisions they had made. And sometimes they were fully defiant, as though daring any soul to question the choices they had made that led them to the point of where they were now. But in the end, they all saddened me and left me speechless for a time.

My thoughts always circling back to the question, "What happened?" What sequence of events took place that caused that person to start believing that was okay, and then acceptable, and finally, the path they wanted to openly choose? "What happened?" Sometimes these people were passing acquaintances, and apart from social media, I knew very little about them. So, when they made such declarations, I was saddened to see them, but I knew so little about them I wondered what had happened but knew there was far more to the story. Perhaps the hard circumstances of life had been too much for them, and they had reacted to life by choosing what seemed right in the moment, but in end, it would lead to heartbreak and ultimately death.

But sometimes I knew the person, once upon a time we had gone to church together, or school, or camp, etc. I had taken the time to get to know them as more than a passing acquaintance and knew they had been given more information, more than just a passing education on life topics, and good direction. We had experienced some significant life events together. We had formed memories and had stories to tell. "What happened?" "Why?" "What was the catalyst for this decision?" I knew some of them knew better. We had sat under the same instruction, and we had started on a similar path, yet a small deviation on the path, in the beginning, led to an entirely different destination shortly after. I always come back to "What happened?" And often, I don't know. Sometimes, they don't know. But not knowing drives me slightly crazy at times. It's not that I want the full story behind each bad decision, I'm not encouraging gossip, and honestly, it would not change the outcome. But it's the desire to both avoid the outcome and consequences this person was now living and to hopefully, help others to do the same. But each story was so different. Different people, often from different backgrounds, with varying life stories, and sometimes opposing views. I was looking for a pattern but finding one was proving elusive.

"What happened?" What was the first thought that person had that made them think, "I want to try that?" Or "This won't hurt anybody". Or, possibly my least favorite "It looks like fun, why shouldn't I try it." "Why shouldn't you try it? Because it will cost you everything!" I have arguments with these different people in my head, trying to reason out why they thought this was alright, and always I come back to the hard truth that sin may be fun for a season, but it will take you farther than you wanted to go, and cost you more than you were willing to pay. Sin is never satisfied with a little when it can go for more. Sin seeks to devour each life it gets its grimy claws into. Proverbs 14:12 address this, "There is a way that appears to be right, but in the end, it leads to death."[1] Sin will cost you everything, and it will lead you down to death. I have seen this over and over, I've seen marriages implode,

1. Prov 14:12 (NIV).

friendships dissolve, companies falter, lives crash and burn, families torn apart, and often innocent people around them then having to live with the consequences of other people's choices. And the odds are, as you are reading this, you are probably thinking of people you know who would fit these descriptions as well. "What happened?"

The answer to this question is often multilayered, full of complexity, and multiple stages of decisions made, yet I can say with confidence, it all starts with a thought. And thoughts can be amazing things. Great ideas that come to life first start as one thought, followed by another thought, then another, and before you realize it, a cascade of thoughts has poured through your mind like rapids over a waterfall. Thoughts can come fast, and slow, sometimes wanted, and sometimes unwanted. Thoughts can build on a previous thought and sometimes spark entirely new thoughts. There is a great deal we are still learning about thoughts, but one thing I do know, everything starts with a thought.

At the root of everything is a thought. Everything done, every word said, every move made, and every decision will start with a thought in one's mind. Francis Schaeffer argued, "Concerning man there is a body, and there is a real, external world. But the thoughts are first, and they are central. So this is where true spirituality in the Christian life rests: in the realm of my thought–life."[2] In one's thought life, or mind is where everything has its beginning. Schaeffer suggests that Romans 1:22–29 demonstrates the order established. As shown in verse 22, "Although they claimed to be wise, they became fools,"[3] this is an internal process; what follows in verse 24 is the external response.[4] "Therefore God gave them over in the sinful desires of their hearts to sexual impurity for the degrading of their bodies with one another."[5] Schaeffer argues from this verse we can observe how the internal process moved to the external response. "Thus we see the order: first there was an

2. Schaeffer, *True Spirituality*, ch. 9, loc. 2333 of 3343.

3. Rom 1:21–29 (NIV).

4. Schaeffer, *True Spirituality*, ch. 9, loc. 2128 of 3343.

5. Rom 1:24 (NIV).

idea in their thought–life, and then came the outward result of the idea."[6] The results or consequences follow the decisions made. Dr. Caroline Leaf argues, "It is with our phenomenal minds that we understand the truths set down in our spirits. It is with our minds that we wire these truths into the brain, which is a part of the body. It is with our minds that we choose to develop the spiritual parts of who we are." Dr. Leaf points to James 1:21 as the inspiration to follow. "Therefore, get rid of all moral filth and the evil that is so prevalent and humbly accept the word planted in you, which can save you."[7]

Rick Nañez, in his book *Full Gospel, Fractured Minds?* succinctly states what he thinks should be the goal for one's mind, "Balance is the bulls–eye at which we are to aim: loving God with body, spirit, and mind."[8] 2 Timothy 1:7 encourages readers by reminding them of what God has given them to help in this, "For God has not given us a spirit of fear, but of power and of love and of a sound mind."[9] Therefore, it is vitally important to develop a sound mind because every part of one's life will be affected by it. Pauletta Otis suggests, "A sound mind is predicated by a deep knowledge of Scripture so that Christians may not be ashamed of nor shame the Gospel."[10] In addition to this, William Robinson, while reviewing the book *How to Keep a Sound Mind*, notes, "Conscious effort can be used in gaining understanding of one's own emotional life and in the establishment of habits and patterns which further mental health."[11] I would postulate that the best definition of a sound mind is in a combination of Otis' and Robinson's descriptions, in addition to 2 Timothy 1:7. Therefore, a sound mind is defined as having in–depth knowledge of scripture with the ability to make a conscious effort to understand one's own emotions and establish habits and patterns to enhance one's

6. Schaeffer, *True Spirituality*, ch. 9, loc. 2128 of 3343.

7. Jas 1:21 (NIV).

8. Nañaz, *Full Gospel Fractured Minds*, 87.

9. 2 Tim 1:7 (NKJV).

10. Otis, "Responding to Religious Violence," 37.

11. Robinson, "How to Keep a Sound Mind," 55.

mental health, including things that keep the brain healthy. At the same time, understanding that love, power, and a sound mind work together as gifts from God and noting that the spirit of fear is in direct opposition to these. "Fear, on the other hand, is distorted love. It is the opposite of love, just as ingratitude is the opposite of gratitude and cruelty is the opposite of kindness. Fear eats away at us, crippling our ability to live the kind of life we want to live."[12] Developing a sound mind requires recognizing the areas in our life that are controlled by fear, and learning how to conquer fear.

With all the previously stated ideas in mind, this book will endeavor to also develop a better understanding of neurotheology. Carrie Doehring argues that "Neurotheology uses neuroscientific data from brain scans of people engaging in religious or spiritual practices like meditation in order to (1) understand what is going on in the brain during religious experiences, (2) raise theological questions, and in some cases, (3) make theological propositions based on this data."[13] Studying neurotheology helps to build an understanding of the need to have a theology of a sound mind.

The purpose of this book is to develop a theology of a sound mind. Nañez defines theology as "thought that deals with the nature of God and his relationship to creation . . . in a nutshell, doing theology is the act of loving the one true God with all one's mind for the sake of magnifying him (i.e., making him large) in everyday life."[14] Developing a theology of a sound mind is significant because the mind is bombarded with constant stimuli fighting for our attention, and no one will accidentally develop a sound mind. Jena Pincott, in her article "Wicked Thoughts," cites a study done by a psychologist at the University of Minnesota about thoughts.

> Within a 16–hour day, he found, people have about 500 thoughts that are unintentional and "intrusive" and that last about 14 seconds on average. While most dealt with the concerns of everyday life, 18 percent were unacceptable, uncomfortable, or just plain bad—politically

12. Leaf, *Think, Learn, Succeed*, ch. 1, loc. 607 of 5409.
13. Doehring, "Minding the Gap," 95.
14. Nañez, *Full Gospel Fractured Minds?*, 157.

> incorrect or mean thoughts. A remaining 13 percent
> were ugly, out of character, or downright shocking—say,
> murderous or perverse ideas.[15]

Thoughts are essential, and the things one allows one's mind to think about matters. Developing a sound mind takes intentionality and discipline. Schaeffer argues, "Moral battles are not won in the external world first. They are always a result flowing naturally from a cause, and the cause is in the internal world of one's thoughts."[16] Sin has been called a heart issue, but I would contend that it is equally a mind and thought issue. Nañez suggests that "We wage war for men's souls but ignore the battle for men's minds."[17] In one's mind, one first entertains a thought and determines if it is permissible to sin or not. In one's mind, battles are waged, and the war on sin is first won or lost. God has fully equipped his people to fight this battle for the mind and to win. The Bible gives multiple directions and instructions on developing a sound mind, and this book will work to cultivate a good theology of a sound mind.

This book's methodology will be a literature review that seeks to understand what research others have conducted on the subject and best practices for the future. In developing a theology of a sound mind, it is crucial to have a more holistic understanding of different aspects of maintaining a sound mind and how they affect our minds, thoughts, and actions. It is also of value to understand how to apply all that is learned to live more fully for Christ and to share what was learned to help others do the same.

A recent study conducted by Timothy Wilson at the University of Virginia and Harvard noted that several participants, ages eighteen to seventy-seven struggled to spend six to fifteen minutes alone with their thoughts with nothing to do but daydream, ponder, and contemplate. It was considered to be an unpleasant experience by the more significant part of the group. "The majority of the participants didn't enjoy being alone with their thoughts, while some preferred even shocking themselves to sitting and

15. Pincott, "WICKED THOUGHTS," 55.
16. Schaeffer, *True Spirituality*, ch. 9, loc. 2182 of 3343.
17. Nañez, *Full Gospel Fractured Minds?*, 224.

thinking."[18] The study found that most participants would rather be doing something negative than not doing something at all, instead of relying on their imaginations for a short while.[19] Learning to be alone with one's thoughts is a critical life skill that needs to be developed, and one way to do that is to understand the need for a sound mind and some of the ways to achieve it.

One can do various things to help develop a sound mind, and this book will focus on four primary areas as they relate to developing a theology of a sound mind. The first thing is the need to focus. Everything else would be superfluous without the ability to focus on the goal one is setting; for this reason, focus comes first. Next, one proven way to improve focus and brain health is through meditation; therefore, the next chapter will look at meditation and what the Bible and different sources have to say. After that, this book will explore the importance of diet and exercise on the mind and how what one consumes directly affects one's ability to think and process. Next, the importance of rest and relaxation as a way for the mind to process and unwind more effectively, to be better prepared for the future, and develop a sound mind. Finally, this book will examine what the information researched entails and how to utilize it and put it into practice.

18. Leaf, *Think, Learn, Succeed*, ch. 2, loc. 648 of 5409.
19. Leaf, *Think, Learn, Succeed*, ch. 2, loc. 648 of 5409.

1

Focus

> We demolish arguments and every pretension that sets
> itself up against the knowledge of God, and we take
> captive every thought to make it obedient to Christ.
>
> —2 CORINTHIANS 3:5

"KEEP YOUR EYE ON the ball." I distinctly remember my father saying this to me over and over as he was trying to teach me how to play baseball, specifically how to hit the ball when I was up to bat. This saying may seem trite at first, but I dare you to try to hit an incoming ball with your bat without watching it very closely, it would be nearly impossible, and unnecessarily dangerous to do so. I can confirm, even when playing tee ball, where the ball is stationary if you don't keep your eye on the ball, you are going to have a rough game. The phrase "keep your eye on the ball" has become synonymous with focus for a reason. If you want to hit the ball and succeed in the game, you're going to have to give it your full attention.

Daniel Goleman, in his book *Focus: The Hidden Driver of Excellence,* quotes William James, a founder of modern psychology, who defined attention as, "The sudden taking possession by the mind, in clear and vivid form, of one of what seems several simultaneously possible objects or trains of thought."[1] To focus or give attention to something is an act of the will and a choice one makes. The writer of Proverbs conveys this need to give one's focus and attention with care intentionally.

> My son, if you accept my words and store up my commands within you, turning your ear to wisdom and applying your heart to understanding—indeed, if you call out for insight and cry aloud for understanding, and if you look for it as for silver and search for it as for hidden treasure, then you will understand the fear of the Lord and find the knowledge of God.[2]

The writer of Proverbs urges the reader with verbs such as turn, apply, call, cry, look, and search, showing that attention requires action. William James seems to agree that focused attention requires action; in some of his writings, he uses phrases such as 'taking possession.'[3] Jason Selk and Ellen Reed, in their book *Relentless Solution Focus: Train Your Mind to Conquer Stress, Pressure, and Underperformance*, argue that "You can talk about it, read about it, teach it all day long, and know what you should be doing, but mental toughness requires that you do something."[4] The need for action cannot be overlooked.

The quest for a theology of a sound mind is not new but has been something various people, such as Saint Augustine of Hippo, have wrestled with and concluded that focus is a necessary starting component. While looking at the theology in Saint Augustine of Hippo's *De Trinitate*, Daniel Simmons quotes Augustine, saying, "What we bring to mind and the way we bring it to mind are important—our minds are actually joined to and formed by those things on which we focus."[5] Augustine exhorts his readers to think

1. Goleman, *Focus: The Hidden Driver,* ch. 1, loc 219 of 5627.
2. Prov 2:1–5 (NIV).
3. Goleman, *Focus: The Hidden Driver*, ch. 1, loc. 219 of 5627.
4. Selk and Reed, *Relentless Solution Focus,* Preface, loc. 209 of 536.
5. Simmons, "We Shall Be like Him," 259.

about God, and in the process, the mind will automatically move in the right direction. "In trying to think of God more clearly, our minds are further joined to, become desirous of, and enjoy God, because this activity is a movement of love. Where the mind seeks after and clings to the things of this world, it revolts against its nature and is dragged down into sin and carnality, 'not by being what they are but by thinking it is.'"[6] Augustine understood both the necessity of focusing our thoughts on God and choosing where to focus our minds.

Dr. Caroline Leaf agrees in her book *Switch On Your Brain* that focus is one of the first steps to living free of this world's burdens and the need to discipline one's thoughts and get them under control. "When you objectively observe your own thinking with the view to capturing rogue thoughts, you in effect direct your attention to stop the negative impact and rewire healthy new circuits in your brain."[7] Dr. Leaf references 2 Corinthians 10:3–5 to show where the Bible already emphasizes the need to do this. "We demolish arguments and every pretension that sets itself up against the knowledge of God, and we take captive every thought to make it obedient to Christ."[8] We need to focus and take our thoughts captive and not let them run wild. The second part of the verse extols the reader to "make it obedient to Christ." Obedience to Christ becomes key in where one should focus. How can one know what it takes to be obedient to Christ? By focusing one's attention on the Bible and what it directs us to do. J. Ellsworth Kalas, in his book *Preaching in an Age of Distraction*, advises the reader to be careful about where one gives their attention. "And as the rule of learning reminds us, what gets our attention gets us."[9] Also, while focusing, one should be aware of the focusing illusion. The focusing illusion is when one focuses overly on a single factor in life, overvaluing the impact of the thing that has the main focus.[10] Focus is good,

---

6. Simmons, "We Shall Be like Him," 259.

7. Leaf, *Switch On Your Brain*, 72.

8. 2 Cor 10:3–5 (NIV).

9. Kalas, *Preaching in an Age of Distraction*, ch. 1, loc. 77 of 2150.

10. Kaczmarek et al., "A Focusing Illusion," 357.

but when one focuses intently on a single aspect of their life, it can cause the other parts of one's life to seem skewed by comparison or that single thing to seem overly important and imbalanced.

It is also beneficial to note the different views on multitasking, as it requires one to focus on multiple things simultaneously. Jeffery Dance and Robert Service, in their article looking at workplace distractions, declared, "Indeed, no one can 'effectively' multitask, for multitasking significantly reduces efficiency, quality, or effectiveness."[11] While in contrast, Chérif Lobna, Valerie Wood, Alexandre Marois, Katherine Labonté, and François Vachon, while studying multitasking in the military, argued, "Many studies show that individuals can differ greatly on their ability to perform while multitasking. Watson and Strayer have shown that some individuals—identified as 'supertaskers'—can perform multiple tasks at the same time without compromising their performance on any particular task."[12] The authors argued that various jobs require multitasking; as such, it should be a skill that is refined, not ignored, with hopes that it will improve. Multitasking can be done with intentional focus, but it depends on each person and their abilities regarding multitasking effectiveness.

When determining what one chooses to focus on, a question to ask oneself would be, 'Is the thing you are focusing on worth giving yourself to?' Dr. Leaf argues that the things one thinks about the most will grow.[13] Brian Fikkert and Kelly Kapic suggest in their book *Becoming Whole* that the things that hold one's attention and captivate them get one's focus, and the things that get one's attention and focus are what they will become like and reflect.[14] So is the thing being thought about worth giving oneself to, worth growing, and worth enhancing in one's life? Dr. Leaf argues that we are solely responsible for where we choose to focus.[15] Each person has the ability to choose what they will focus their attention on at

11. Dance and Service, "Attractive Nuisance," 35.
12. Chérif et al., "Multitasking in the Military," 433.
13. Leaf, *Think, Learn, Succeed*, ch. 4, loc. 620 or 5409.
14. Fikkert and Kappic, *Becoming Whole*, 52.
15. Leaf, *Switch On Your Brain*, 45.

all times, and in turn, what they will become like and reflect. Thus, it is crucial to intentionally focus on things that have worth and value to help build a sound mind.

"Yikes, I did not mean to see that," I have had that thought more times than I can count for various reasons. Sometimes it is because I was scrolling on social media and something popped up on my feed that I did not want to see. Or while watching a show, or movie, suddenly the scene changes, and it is not for the best. Or, sometimes there are advertisements around me, whether walking while shopping, or sometimes while driving. It seems to be an inevitability, running into these images that would be better not seen. And then what do you do with that thought? You take it captive! "For though we live in the world, we do not wage war as the world does. The weapons we fight with are not the weapons of the world. On the contrary, they have divine power to demolish strongholds. We demolish arguments and every pretension that sets itself up against the knowledge of God, and we take captive every thought to make it obedient to Christ."[16] I'm hoping by this point in the book you are feeling empowered with the amazing reality that you get to decide what you are thinking about all the time. Even if you are interrupted by an image that you wish you had not seen, you get to decide if that image gets to take up your mental real-estate. Just because you saw it, does not mean it gets to spend time on your frequently played list of mental images. This also goes with what you read. This issue seems just as pervasive in literature as it is everywhere else. There is a battle going on for our minds, and the good news, it is a fight we can win. "For God has not given us a spirit of fear, but of power and of love and of a sound mind."[17] When you take your thoughts captive you make a declaration that you are not going to passively allow just anything in your thought processes, you get to decide to honor God with the very thoughts in your mind.

I enjoy going exploring, and seeing new things, but as I've traveled, whether by foot, bike, ski, boat, car, jeep, or truck, I've

16. 2 Cor 10:3–5 (NIV).
17. 2 Tim 1:7 (NKJV).

learned, often the hard way, there are places I should not go. This is not meant as a restrictive ruling keeping me from fun, rather it is a safety warning, because going there could cause serious injury. While skiing there are signs posted for places one should not venture, it's not that they want to keep the skiers from fun, but they want to keep them from dangerous situations. And if you have ever been off-roading, you may have experienced this as well. Though off-roading usually means there are no signs posted, instead the driver must be even more vigilant, so they don't drive themselves into a serious problem. As the driver becomes more experienced, they usually become more aware of their surroundings, and of potential pitfalls ahead, and they learn to avoid them. Depending on the area, a vehicle can be totaled while attempting some off-roading obstacles. As one gains awareness that the problem areas will just slow them down, thereby keeping them from their actual destination, which is usually far more enjoyable in the long run, one becomes more attentive to the path taken. Interestingly, our thought processes are very similar. As we learn to focus and take our thoughts captive, we learn the warning signs of places we should not let our minds go, and some to entirely avoid. Much like a road that is no longer safe to traverse. If you know you are going to get stuck in a certain place, don't go there, and don't let your thoughts go there either. This works in the positive as well, as we train our minds on what to focus on, we start to identify roads and paths that are not only safe but are also beneficial and good for us to travel. If you have ever struggled with your thought life, it's not too late to start taking your thoughts captive and choosing where to focus instead.

Healthy Habits to Build Focus

Focus has been identified as a necessity for developing a good theology of a sound mind; without focus, a sound mind would be unattainable. Selk and Reed, when researching what they deemed the most successful people; noted that, "Instead of allowing their mind to focus on everything they didn't have or couldn't do, the most successful people have learned to direct their thoughts in a manner that produces positive emotions and productive actions."[18] The ability to focus one's thoughts to move forward is of utmost importance. Practical ways to implement different habits into one's daily life are necessary to become more focused. Fikkert and Kapic recommend not just rejecting what is not beneficial but focusing on what is of value. "In other words, we can't just try to reject the idols of this world. We need to replace these idols with worship of the one true God, immersing our hearts—our minds, affections, and wills—in His beauty and wonder."[19] Each person needs to turn their focus to things that honor God and repeat this process frequently. Dr. Leaf suggests that, "The primary success of capturing your thoughts will be to focus on God's ways first, not the world's ways."[20] Each person can do this more successfully as they know God's ways by studying his word.

The writer of Colossians extols the reader in ways to capture one's thoughts, "Set your minds on things that are above, not on things that are on earth."[21] One should choose to focus on things that please God. Selk and Reed suggest that "It is the focus on solutions instead of problems that is the key to health and success."[22] Philippians 4 gives direction on where one should focus, "Finally, brothers, whatever is true, whatever is honorable, whatever is just, whatever is pure, whatever is lovely, whatever is commendable, if there is any excellence, if there is anything worthy of praise, think about these things."[23] This verse gives clear direction on where to focus one's attention.

One can learn new habits to focus on positive things. Dr. Leaf notes that, "We can retrain the brain to focus on the good things in life. We step into our 'normal' when we do this because we are wired for love. Having an 'attitude of gratitude' enables us

---

18. Selk and Reed, *Relentless Solution Focus*, Intro. Loc. 254 of 536.

19. Fikkert and Kappic, *Becoming Whole*, 65.

20. Leaf, *Switch On Your Brain*, 73.

21. Col 3:2 (NIV).

22. Selk and Reed, *Relentless Solution Focus*, Intro. Loc. 268 of 536.

23. Phil 4:8 (NIV).

to see more possibilities, to feel more energy, and to succeed at higher levels in our lives."[24] Focusing on the positive things that one is grateful for can improve one's awareness of the positive things in their life.

On a physical note, to help with focus, stay hydrated; Carter and Carter argue that "Dehydration has many negative health ramifications. These include trouble sleeping, short–term memory loss, difficulty staying focused and processing logical problems, energy loss, and, in more severe cases, it may be a factor in the on-set of Alzheimer's, Parkinson's, and Lou Gehrig's disease."[25] From the above information, one can deduce the need to focus, some different things to focus on, and things to do to improve one's ability to focus as it is necessary to build a strong mind. One way to improve one's focus is through meditation.

24. Leaf, *Think, Learn, Succeed*, ch. 1, loc. 607 of 5409.
25. Carter and Carter, *Morning Mind*, ch. 5, loc. 1123 of 4183.

2

Meditation

> May these words of my mouth and this
> meditation of my heart be pleasing in your
> sight, Lord, my Rock and my Redeemer.
>
> —PSALM 19:14

MEDITATION IS IN ESSENCE, dwelling on something. And, if there is one thing I'm good at, it's dwelling on stuff. I don't know about you, but I have certainly spent my fair share of time thinking about, dwelling on, and in general, obsessing over things. I will give you an example. I could pick any of a dozen conversations I've had with people, especially arguments, and demonstrate how I'm very good at thinking and dwelling on them for the foreseeable future. The conversation may have lasted only a few minutes, but I will think about, rehash, and reargue with myself these conversations repeatedly. I also do this with compliments and congratulations. I will consider the information from many angles, trying to decipher if there is a deeper meaning, or if that was all there was to it. If you have ever done this, you are in good company, and inadvertently are already set up to practice meditation. Though there are many forms of meditation, some are far more beneficial than others.

Meditation is an ancient tradition focused on contemplation that is gaining new acceptance in the culture today. Edmund Clowney argues that one can observe meditations in the Old Testament. "Meditation is spoken of most often in the poetry and wisdom sayings of the Old Testament. Psalms and Proverbs not only speak meditation—they are written meditations."[1] Meditation can be internal in focusing the mind and external by participating in journaling, singing, and chanting. James Finley suggests that Saint Benedict gave directions on meditation, "Benedict wrote a Rule prescribing a way of life in which the chanting of the psalms in the monastic choir, manual labor, and everything the monk or nun does is to become a meditation. Which is to say, everything becomes a way of entering into a more interior, meditative awareness of oneness with God."[2] Meditation is a natural inclination of the mind.[3] Carter and Carter argue that "Meditation can also increase feel–good neurotransmitters like dopamine and serotonin, known as the 'happiness hormone,' allowing us to come back to a more balanced and peaceful mental and emotional state."[4] Inadvertently, one can meditate and fixate on different things throughout the day without realizing it, which is why being aware of one's thoughts is vital.

To help develop a sound mind, one should intentionally build meditation into their daily life. Dr. Leaf argues that, "Science is showing that meditation on the elements of Jesus's teachings rewires healthy new circuits in the brain."[5] Choosing to focus on God and his word has many benefits. Joshua extols the Israelites to mediate as well. "Keep this Book of the Law always on your lips; meditate on it day and night, so that you may be careful to do everything written in it. Then you will be prosperous and

1. Clowney, *Christian Meditation*, 19.
2. Finley, *Christian Meditation*, 4.
3. "Merriam–Webster, "Meditate."
4. Carter and Carter, *The Morning Mind*, Intro. Loc. 390 of 4183.
5. Leaf, *Switch On Your Brain*, 73.

successful."[6] David also encourages his readers to meditate on the law of the Lord in the book of Psalms.[7] Joshua, David, and Leaf acknowledge that meditation has immense value. What one meditates on is essential, so important that they gave specific examples of what one should focus on while meditating. However, Andrew Newberg and Mark Robert Waldman would argue that what one meditates on is not as important as the act of meditating itself. "Contemplating God will change your brain, but I want to point out that meditation on other grand themes will also change your brain. If you contemplate the Big Bang, or immerse yourself in the study of evolution—or choose to play a musical instrument, for that matter—you'll change the neural circuitry in ways that enhance your cognitive health."[8] Sanjay Gupta would agree that meditation enhances one's brain. ". . . it is clear that with various behavior interventions such as meditation training or regular sound sleep, our brains can be put into hyperdrive status . . ."[9] Meditation has proven value in helping to improve the brain and strengthen the mind.

While meditation is understood to help the brain, the debate continues about what kind of meditation. Newberg and Waldman are proponents of a specific type of meditation called Kirtan Kriya, this technique comes from India and focuses on breathing and repeating a mantra of sounds, such as 'sa,' 'ta,' 'na,' and 'ma,' and a specific movement of fingers called mudras.[10] Clowney contrasts this with Christian meditation, "Not an arbitrary 'mantra' but the rich treasure of Scripture is the key to Christian meditation."[11] Newberg and Waldman acknowledge that contemplating spiritual things, not just sounds, has been proven to change the brain, "but religious and spiritual contemplation changes your brain in a profoundly different way because it strengthens a unique neural

---

6. Josh 1:8 (NIV).

7. Ps 1:1–3 (NIV).

8. Newberg and Waldman, *How GOD Changes Your Brain*, 15.

9. Gupta, *Keep Sharp: Build a Better Brain at Any Age*, ch. 1, loc. 292 of 642.

10. Newberg and Waldman, *How GOD Changes Your Brain*, 23–24.

11. Clowney, *Christian Meditation*, 23.

circuit that specifically enhances social awareness and empathy while subduing destructive feelings and emotions."[12] There are many forms of meditation that one can participate in; the question becomes, what does one want the outcome to be? For some following more Eastern philosophies, the desired outcome is a sense of nothingness. "You are attempting to achieve absolute inner silence. No emotions or thoughts—just pure awareness or consciousness of what is."[13] Though Newberg and Waldman admit in their studies, not many achieve this outcome of nothingness, and no emotions or thoughts or pure awareness.[14] Clowney argues that "The oneness with the absolute that the Maharishi pictures as the goal of human destiny is really the opposite of Christian fellowship with the living God. It is not the experience of *knowing* God but the delusion of *being* God."[15] What one chooses to meditate on is vitally important.

John Main suggests that Christian meditation has a loftier goal than nothingness, but to become aware of God in everything. "The all–important aim in Christian meditation is to allow God's mysterious and silent presence within us to become more and more not only *a* reality, but *the* reality in our lives; to let it become that reality which gives meaning, shape and purpose to everything we do, to everything we are."[16] Meditating on God and his word helps to sharpen our minds. Dr. Leaf argues that those who meditate regularly have shown that parts of their brain are more active than those who do not meditate; this is demonstrated in higher intelligence, wisdom, and feeling at peace.[17] The choice to meditate on God and his word has a sound foundation of benefits that have been proven to help build a sound mind.

What we choose to meditate on matters. Recently I experienced this on a whole new level, someone very close to me had a

12. Newberg and Waldman, *How GOD Changes Your Brain*, 14.

13. Newberg and Waldman, *How GOD Changes Your Brain*, 212.

14. Newberg and Waldman, *How GOD Changes Your Brain*, 212.

15. Clowney, *Christian Meditation*, 9.

16. Main, *Word into Silence*, 4.

17. Leaf, *Switch On Your Brain*, 84.

health scare and it changed my perspective on so many things in an instant. Some of the things I had been focused on, and somewhat meditating on quickly fell away, and new things immediately took their place. My focus shifted and I almost instantly started obsessing and inadvertently meditating on all the "what ifs," and it started to drive me crazy. I have this completely unrealistic tendency of trying to figure out every possible outcome to mentally prepare myself for it beforehand. As previously mentioned, it is unrealistic, and ridiculous. There are far too many variables in life, which compounds into infinite possible outcomes. I recognized that I could not focus all my attention on the "what ifs" and still have peace in the middle of it all. I had to refocus my thoughts very intentionally and meditate on the word of God.

It was not an easy choice, but it was a good choice. When I intentionally captured my wayward thoughts that kept tending towards worry and fear, and chose to pray and meditate on the word of God it helped immensely. It is not that the situation automatically changed, because it didn't, but I changed while I was in that situation. I had to consciencely chose what I was going to focus and mediate on often, sometimes it was minute-by-minute, and sometimes it was every hour. Some of the things I did to help during that time were to watch a movie that expounded on the greatness of God, I spent a lot of time talking to God in prayer, dug into the word of God with a whole new intentionality, and listened to lots of worship songs, and also sang along. The Psalms became one of my go-to books of the Bible during that time. "I lift up my eyes to the mountains—where does my help come from? My help comes from the Lord, the Maker of heaven and earth."[18] Also, Psalm 46 "God is our refuge and strength, an ever-present help in trouble."[19] I was not perfect at this by any means, but as I put this into practice, I started getting faster at refocusing my thoughts and meditating on the word of God. I was careful with what I was meditating on because I could tell it was making a huge difference. I did not particularly enjoy the experience, but I do admit it helped

18. Ps 121:1–2 (NIV).
19. Ps 46:1 (NIV).

to continue to grow a healthy habit of choosing what to meditate on, even when it is especially challenging in the process.

Healthy Habits to Incorporate Meditation

Meditation is good for the brain and helps to build a strong mind. George Hunter explores how the early Celtic church practiced meditation or 'contemplative prayer' as a lifestyle. "The community worshiped together, perhaps twice daily; they learned much of the Scriptures together—by heart—especially the Psalms. They nourished one another in a life of 'contemplative prayer,' . . ."[20] Meditating on scripture and singing worship songs is a form of meditation. Newberg and Waldman encourage longer forms of prayer over shorter ones due to the benefits. "However, when prayer is incorporated into longer forms of intense meditation, or practiced within the context of weekly religious activity, many health benefits have been found, including greater length of life."[21] Leaf recommends prayer as well for meditation. "When we pray, when we catch our thoughts, when we memorize and quote scripture, we move into this deep meditative state."[22] The different aspects of meditation and ways to incorporate them are good to keep in mind.

Clowney argues there are three dimensions of Christian meditation. First, it is grounded in the truth of God, second, it responds to the love of God, and third, these lead the Christian to worship God.[23] Main suggests that "Meditation is a learning process. It is a process of learning to pay attention, to concentrate, to attend."[24] Worshiping with songs and instruments is a common theme among the sources cited as different ways to meditate. The

20. Hunter, *Celtic Way Of Evangelism*, 17.

21. Newberg and Waldman, *How GOD Changes Your Brain*, 28.

22. Leaf, *Switch On Your Brain: The Key to Peak Happiness, Thinking, and Health*, 84.

23. Clowney, *Christian Meditation*, 9.

24. Main, *Word into Silence*, 3.

differences noted are the various types of preferred music.[25] New-berg and Waldman suggest music is good for the brain.

> In one study, musicians who used repeated finger move-ments had lower rates of dementia, and in another, early musical training with children resulted in the 'long-term enhancement of visual-spatial, verbal, and mathematical performance.' In fact, it is fair to consider any musical training a form of cognitive meditation because it involves intense concentration, repetition of instructional techniques, body coordination, and moti-vational attention. There is even considerable evidence documenting the effects of pleasant music on the brain. It deepens emotional experiences, enhances visual and auditory processing, and improves attention and the processing of emotions.[26]

Music is an excellent way to practice meditation, whether playing an instrument, or singing along. Though sometimes it is chal-lenging to focus one's mind on meditation, and a method to help is exercising. Newberg and Waldman argue that exercise can be viewed as a form of meditation as it involves continuous concen-tration and a conscious regulation of breathing and movements.[27] Meditation and exercising both improve the brain and help to build a sound mind.

25. Newberg and Waldman, *How GOD Changes Your Brain*, 35.
26. Newberg and Waldman, *How GOD Changes Your Brain*, 35.
27. Newberg and Waldman, *How GOD Changes Your Brain*, 160.

3

Diet and Exercise

So whether you eat or drink or whatever
you do, do it all for the glory of God.

—1 CORINTHIANS 10:31

DIET AND EXERCISE, THIS infamous duo has caused many a rest-less night for me as I've contemplated the best and most efficient way forward with both. They go hand in hand with living a healthy lifestyle, and wouldn't you know it, in building a sound mind. Typical, I know. But hear me out, if you are a huge fan of eating well and exercising, then this will be a piece of cake, so to speak, and will be easy–to–swallow information. If you are in the process of creating a healthy diet/eating well and getting into exercising, then hopefully this information will be another motivator for you in your journey towards living healthy. And if you have not yet started to eat well, and excise more, then my hope is, armed with this information, you will move towards a better diet/eating well and exercising more, because there is no way around it, it's good for your brain. That being said, please note this is not a diet book with a prescribed way of eating. Though the following chapter will delve into why a good diet and exercise are important, I'm not advocating how that looks for each person, simply that it should be done mindfully. The brain needs nutrients, and it gets that from what is consumed. If we want to develop a sound mind, what is consumed needs to be taken into account, and also how much activity is in each day.

The drive to achieve a sound mind would be incomplete without considering the importance of what one consumes and the quantity of physical movement in one's day, commonly referred to as diet and exercise. Gupta, in his book, *Keep Sharp: Build a Better Brain at Any Age*, argues that, "In order to best take care of your body, you have to first take care of your mind."[1] Romans 12 exhorts us, "Therefore, I urge you, brothers and sisters, in view of God's mercy, to offer your bodies as a living sacrifice, holy and pleasing to God—this is your true and proper worship. Do not conform to the pattern of this world, but be transformed by the renewing of your mind. Then you will be able to test and approve what God's will is—his good, pleasing and perfect will."[2] From these verses, the reader is reminded of essential factors involved in renewing the mind, and these things require action and intention.

Anders Hansen, who wrote, *The Real Happy Pill: Power Up Your Brain by Moving Your Body*, suggests, "Not only do you feel better when you're physically active; your concentration, memory, creativity, and resistance to stress are also affected. You're able to process information more quickly—so you think faster—and become more adept at mobilizing intellectual resources as needed."[3] Exercise helps to improve the mind in multiple ways. In his article "Optimizing Brain Health," John Miller agrees that exercise plays a vital role in keeping the brain healthy. "The benefits of aerobic exercise to the brain are enumerated, including improved cognitive functioning, greater sense of well–being and decreased

---

1. Gupta, *Keep Sharp*, ch. 1, loc. 148 of 642.

2. Rom 12:1–2 (NIV).

3. Hansen, *Real Happy Pill*, ch. 1, loc. 65 of 423.

depression."[4] The benefits of exercise impact the mind in multiple ways. Newberg and Waldman argue that "Vigorous exercise strengthens every part of the brain, as well as what it is connected to—the body."[5] There are so many advantages to exercising for your whole body. Newberg and Waldman expound upon the various benefits.

> All forms of exercise enhance neural performance and rebuild damaged circuits caused by brain lesions and strokes. Exercise improves cognition and academic performance. It repairs and protects you from the neurological damage caused by stress. It enhances brain plasticity. It boosts immune function. It reduces anxiety. It can be used to treat clinical depression, and it is just as effective as antidepressants. In fact, for older patients, exercise is equivalent to twelve sessions of psychodynamic psychotherapy. It slows down the loss of brain tissue as you age, protects you from Alzheimer's disease, and reduces your vulnerability to chronic illness.[6]

The body and mind were created to extract benefits from exercising. 1 Timothy 4 reminds the reader, "For physical training is of some value, but godliness has value for all things, holding promise for both the present life and the life to come."[7] While godliness has the greater value, exercise and physical training have value and should not be discarded. Henry Thoreau, the famous American essayist, understood the need to exercise to improve his mind and writing and he put it so well, "How vain it is to sit down to write when you have not stood up to live! Methinks that the moment my legs begin to move my thoughts begin to flow—as if I had given vent to the stream at the lower end and consequently new fountains flowed into it at the upper."[8] Thoreau understood the value of movement and how it helped him get his thoughts moving.

4. Miller, "Optimizing Brain Health," 3.

5. Newberg and Waldman, *How GOD Changes Your Brain*, 160–61.

6. Newberg and Waldman, *How GOD Changes Your Brain*, 160–61.

7. 1 Tim 4:8 (NIV).

8. Hodder, *Thoreau's Ecstatic Witness*, 285.

Being aware of one's diet and how the food consumed will impact the mind's ability to function at an optimal level is also quite helpful. Dr. Leaf argues in her book *Think & Eat Yourself Smart*, "Although your brain is only 2 percent of the weight of your body, it consumes 20 percent of the total energy (oxygen) and 65 percent of the glucose—what you eat will directly affect the brain's ability to function on a significant scale . . . how and what we eat affects our mind, brain, and body."[9] The impact on the brain is one reason one needs to be conscientious of what one is eating. Dr. Leaf argues that God desires us to be healthy in all areas, our spirits, souls, and bodies; all three are vital and are designed to work in an integrated fashion, motivating and cyclically stimulating each other.[10] When one area is ignored or forgotten, one can no longer function at an optimal level.

The book of 1 Corinthians would appear to agree with the necessity of honoring God with all the parts of one's life. "Do you not know that your bodies are temples of the Holy Spirit, who is in you, whom you have received from God? You are not your own; you were bought at a price. Therefore honor God with your bodies."[11] The book of 1 Thessalonians would also seem to concur with this assessment. "May God himself, the God of peace, sanctify you through and through. May your whole spirit, soul and body be kept blameless at the coming of our Lord Jesus Christ."[12] Gupta, who is not approaching the concept of building a better brain from a Christian perspective, still noted, "I have also been exploring the deep connection between the heart and the brain. It is true that what is good for one is also good for the other, but I now believe the secret is that it all begins with your brain."[13] All the components, one's spirit, soul, and body, were designed to work together, and they are at their best when they do. 3 John extols the reader, "Dear friend, I pray that you may enjoy good health and

9. Leaf, *Think & Eat Yourself Smart*, 84–85.

10. Leaf, *Think & Eat Yourself Smart*, 85.

11. 1 Cor 6:19–20 (NIV).

12. 1 Thess 5:23 (NIV).

13. Gupta, *Keep Sharp*, ch. 1, loc. 148 of 642.

that all may go well with you, even as your soul is getting along well."[14] John touches on the importance of integration of the different components that make up each person.

Darin Olien notes the remarkable truth that our bodies convert what we eat into what our bodies need, "Turning water into wine is a miracle, no doubt. But is it more miraculous than turning broccoli, walnuts, beets, apples, and water into bones and organs and blood and brains?"[15] The body's ability to convert food into what it requires is impressive. Lisa Mosconi, the author of *Brain Food*, argues, "The health of our brains, and our capacity to adapt and survive, is intrinsically dependent on our diet—and therefore our environment."[16] Our diet is a crucial component of developing a sound mind. Mosconi also suggests we have more control than we are aware of, claiming, "The truth is, we have more power than we realize. The power of our personal choices often remains untapped because of conventional Western medicine's tendency to treat symptoms with drugs or surgery before considering less risky and oftentimes more effective approaches instead—like eating better."[17] Deuteronomy reminds the reader of the responsibility of their personal choices. "This day I call the heavens and the earth as witnesses against you that I have set before you life and death, blessings and curses. Now choose life, so that you and your children may live and that you may love the Lord your God, listen to his voice, and hold fast to him . . ."[18] We must focus on what we want and work towards it. We have power over our choices and get to choose life, what an awesome privilege. David Perlmutter and Kristin Loberg, in their book *Brain Maker: The Power of Gut Microbes to Heal and Protect Your Brain for Life*, argue that what one consumes has a profound effect on the brain. "The digestive system is intimately connected to what goes on in the brain."[19] To

14. 3 John 1:2 (NIV).
15. Olien, *SuperLife*, Intro. Loc. 58 of 592.
16. Mosconi, *Brain Food*, ch. 1, loc. 437 of 708.
17. Mosconi, *Brain Food*, ch. 1, loc. 286 of 708.
18. Deut 30:19–20 (NIV).
19. Perlmutter and Loberg, *Brain Maker*, ch. 1, loc. 133 of 512.

achieve a sound mind, one must be attentive to what one is consuming as it directly affects the body and the mind.

There are varying opinions on what best lifestyle choices and habits are available. J.Z. Parker, who wrote *Bible Diet, An Apple A Day*, argues that "One book, the Bible, is the first to deal with nutrition and what and how to eat. One would then think that countries whose population is predominantly Christian would logically have for its citizenry very healthy individuals: neither skinny nor fat, neither starving nor overweight. The question then follows: are such countries following the biblical advice on diet?"[20] In contrast, Lois Tverberg argues, "Of course God wants us to be healthy and would be pleased if some of us took off a few excess pounds. But it's important not to extract lessons from the Bible that it never intended to teach. To search the Bible for secrets for slimming down is to read it upside down and backward of what it meant in its time."[21] In developing a theology of a sound mind, the goal is to understand the principles of a good diet and our need for exercise and how they benefit the mind, not prescribing what each person should do.

Exercising and movement help me focus and I know it. Sometimes when I get stuck while working on something, whether that is writing or another project, I will get up and do something else for a time. Sometimes that looks like cleaning something, or organizing, or going for walk or bike ride. Either way, I know that movement helps me focus and helps me process. Sometimes while moving around my jumbled thoughts seem to straighten themselves into more coherent concepts and sentences. It is nice to know that when we are exercising it is not only beneficial to our physical health, but also the health of our minds as well.

20. Parker, *Bible Diet, An Apple A Day*, 7.
21. Tverberg, *Reading the Bible with Rabbi Jesus*, ch. 2, loc. 409 of 4716.

Healthy Habits of Diet and Exercise

A good diet and exercise are beneficial for the brain, and in turn, help to produce a strong mind. Dr. Todd Strong suggests, "What you eat determines your energy intake, and the kinds of raw materials your body gets to work with—clearly, your brain must be affected by what you eat, as will every other important system or organ in the body like your muscles, skeleton, gut, immune system, heart and blood vessels."[22] A recommended healthy habit would be to choose what one consumes every day mindfully. There are many sources to guide each individual to find the best dietary plan for them, and it all begins with a choice and intentionality. Dr. Leaf suggests incorporating fasting to help strengthen the mind, "Whether it involves skipping one meal or more or excluding certain foods from the diet, fasting has played an important role in human history—spiritually and physically."[23] Fasting helps to reset one's mindset and develops discipline.

Moreover, regarding exercise, Strong argues that an inactive lifestyle that forgoes exercise will have adverse outcomes for overall health. The good news is the result of being reasonably active can have a positive effect.[24] "Being modestly active, engaging in sensible levels of appropriate exercise regularly will confer benefits to your overall health, and support every single organ and system within the body, without exception. Your brain needs exercise, and your brain needs your body to get exercise, especially if it wants to remain healthy, let alone to perform at peak levels."[25] Physical training has value that should be utilized to help support a strong mind. Leaf argues, "We cannot think good food thoughts without sleep, and we can't digest the food we eat well without sleep. Likewise, exercise is equally important. Not only does it make our blood circulate more efficiently through our bodies, bringing the chemicals of life to the cells and removing the debris of

22. Strong, *Reclaim Your Brain*, ch. 1, loc. 309 of 3889.

23. Leaf, *Think & Eat Yourself Smart*, 125.

24. Strong, *Reclaim Your Brain*, ch. 1, loc. 341 of 3889.

25. Strong, *Reclaim Your Brain*, ch. 1, loc. 341 of 3889.

metabolism, but regular exercise also benefits the mind."[26] We need to keep a healthy balance and understand that eating mindfully and exercising are valuable. Getting rest helps improve all of the habits previously mentioned to help build a strong mind.

4

Rest and Relaxation

"Come to me, all you who are weary and burdened,
and I will give you rest. Take my yoke upon you
and learn from me, for I am gentle and humble
in heart, and you will find rest for your souls.
For my yoke is easy and my burden is light."

—MATTHEW 11:28–30

REST AND RELAXATION, EVEN saying those two words together
cause images to pop into my mind of palm trees and water lapping
on the shore. Perhaps a gentle breeze is also blowing, filled with
the scents of salt water mixed with sand, maybe fresh flowers are
growing nearby, and most probably sunscreen has been lathered
on. Ah, what a relaxing place. I have never had a vacation like this,
but popular movies, television, and books make this out to seem
a perfect location, and if only we could all get there, we would all
be able to relax. Of course, if we were all there, it would also be
crowded, but hopefully still relaxing. And while a tropical vacation
would be wonderful, I have learned not to wait until I get there to

start improving my skills in resting and learning to relax. I tend to be focused on what I can be doing and constantly accomplishing. This is great for work but exhausting for my regular home life. Learning to rest well is not about being lazy, but about realizing it is ok to take a break and recharge. This may sound silly, but I have had to learn that resting does not diminish my value or worth. That we are so much more than the sum of our accomplishments.

Rest and relaxation can be used interchangeably, but for this chapter, I have them separated, and you will see why. This seems like such an easy thing to do, it seems quite obvious, but in our driven society, this can be harder than it sounds. I like to relax, I like to think I'm good at it until I actually try to just relax. Then my mind is bombarded with thoughts of all the things I feel like I should be doing instead. So, instead of fully relaxing, I'm fighting the sense that I should be accomplishing something, and that my relaxation is interfering with my productivity. It's hard for me to say I just relaxed over the weekend, but it's easy to list off my accomplishments instead, "I cleaned the house from top to bottom, got the laundry done, tried a new recipe, read a book, etc." But rest and relaxation are important, and sometimes that is just what needs to be accomplished.

Rest and relaxation are common phrases that are generally accepted as essential parts of one's life. However, based on the overwhelming options of and dependence on coffee, energy drinks, energy pills, and the like, we are not taking our need for adequate rest into proper consideration.[1] Relaxation is often referred to as vacation time but is not a standard part of one's routine. Rest and relaxation are related yet separate concepts that affect the body and mind.[2] Dr. Leaf suggests that "Sleep is needed to regenerate and protect the proper biological function of both our bodies and minds and to consolidate memory."[3] Our bodies need rest, how much differs from person to person, but rest is essential.[4]

1. Carter and Carter, *Morning Mind*, ch. 1, loc. 576 of 4183.
2. Gupta, *Keep Sharp*, ch. 1, loc. 353–62 of 642.
3. Leaf, *Think & Eat Yourself Smart*, 206.
4. Strong, *Reclaim Your Brain*, ch. 7, loc. 1983 of 3889.

When considering one's need for rest, Janna Mantua and Rebecca Spencer, in their article "Exploring the Nap Paradox: Are Mid–Day Sleep Bouts a Friend or Foe?" noted that napping could have benefits, yet not for everyone, ". . . in spite of these reported benefits of naps, frequent napping has also been associated with numerous negative outcomes (e.g., cognitive decline, hypertension, diabetes), particularly in older populations."[5] However, Catherine Milner and Kimberly Cote argued in their article "Benefits of Napping in Healthy Adults: impact of nap length, time of day, age, and experience with napping," that "many researchers have confirmed benefits of napping for waking performance . . . Napping also improves mood and subjective levels of sleepiness and fatigue. It is particularly beneficial to performance on tasks, such as addition, logical reasoning, reaction time, and symbol recognition."[6] Napping can be controversial, but researchers seem to agree that it is particular to each person and their genetics on how they will respond to naps.[7]

The Psalms speak about our need for rest, In Psalm 62:1 "Truly my soul finds rest in God; my salvation comes from him."[8] Also, the whole chapter of Psalm 23, is often viewed as full of restful and refreshing verses to encourage one to slow down and just breathe in God's peace.

> The Lord is my shepherd, I lack nothing. He makes me lie down in green pastures, he leads me beside quiet waters, he refreshes my soul. He guides me along the right paths for his name's sake. Even though I walk through the darkest valley, I will fear no evil, for you are with me; your rod and your staff, they comfort me. You prepare a table before me in the presence of my enemies You anoint my head with oil; my cup overflows. Surely your

---

5. Mantua and Spencer, "Exploring the Nap Paradox," 88.

6. Milner and Cote, "Benefits of Napping in Healthy Adults," 273.

7. Hirschlag, "Naps Don't Work for Everyone. Genetic Differences Are Why," *The Washington Post*, March 7, 2020.

8. Ps 62:1 (NIV).

goodness and love will follow me all the days of my life
and I will dwell in the house of the Lord forever.[9]

We can better rest when we trust God to handle whatever is going
on in our lives. And in Psalm 46, "He says, 'Be still, and know that
I am God; I will be exalted among the nations, I will be exalted in
the earth.'"[10] Furthermore, Psalm 127 reminds the readers of the
futility of working oneself to death to gain all that the world offers.
"Unless the Lord builds the house, the builders labor in vain. Unless the Lord watches over the city, the guards stand watch in vain.
In vain you rise early and stay up late, toiling for food to eat—for
he grants sleep to those he loves."[11] These verses all emphasize that
real rest is only found in God. In Matthew, Jesus offers rest to anyone who would come to him when he says "Come to me, all you
who are weary and burdened, and I will give you rest. Take my
yoke upon you and learn from me, for I am gentle and humble in
heart, and you will find rest for your souls. For my yoke is easy and
my burden is light."[12] To be heavily burdened or stressed is not a
new problem, but Jesus offers a simple way to let go of stress and
accept his rest.

Newberg and Waldman argue that stress is a significant
problem and that relaxation helps, "But relaxation does much
more than relieve bodily tension, it interrupts the brain's release of
stress–stimulating neurochemicals, and stress is the number one
killer in America."[13] Relaxation should be an intentional part of
one's day as it is needed. Our lack of rest does not fool the brain;
Michael Steinborn and Lynn Huestegge, when reviewing classic
works on understanding the brain's need for rest, argue that if one
does not get enough rest, the brain will cause mental blocks pur-
posely to get rest.[14] "He considered it almost certain that mental

9. Ps 23:1–6 (NIV).

10. Ps 46:10 (NIV).

11. Ps 127:1–2 (NIV).

12. Matt 11:28–30 (NIV).

13. Newberg and Waldman, *How GOD Changes Your Brain*, 155.

14. Steinborn and Huestegge, "Walk Down the Lane Gives Wings to Your
Brain," 795.

blocks act as enforced micro rest that is inherent in the cognitive system to prevent a more severe decrement from occurring . . . 'the rest afforded by these blocks keep the individual's objective efficiency up to an average level . . . '"[15] If we don't get proper rest our brains will try to get it in other ways. Gupta advocates that, "our everyday experiences, including what we eat, how much we exercise, with whom we socialize, what challenges we face, how well we sleep, and what we do to reduce stress and learn, factor much more into our brain health and overall wellness than we can imagine."[16] Sleep is key to keeping a healthy mind. Strong advises, "Getting good quality sleep, enough sleep, and regular sleep supports health and brain function in many ways."[17] One seems to know this intrinsically, that one needs to get a good night's sleep to function well the following day. In his article "Optimizing Brain Health," Miller argues for the critical role sleep plays in one's life, "It identifies sleep as one of the most important requirements for good brain health."[18] No matter how much one enjoys caffeine stimulants, nothing takes the place of proper rest in helping to encourage a sound mind.

I enjoy coffee a great deal, whether it is hot, or iced, latte, mocha, or americano, macchiato, or cappuccino, French press, drip, or other fancy fru-fru coffees, but I will quickly admit, no matter how delightful coffee can be, it is a poor substitute for a good night's sleep. I have inadvertently tested this many times, and I always wish I would have been more diligent about getting a good night's sleep. Rest is wonderful, and the feeling of being well rested helps one feel more prepared for the challenges of the day that lie ahead. Whenever I think about the need for proper rest, stories of traveling come to mind. Whether by car, van, train, or plane, it can be hard to get a good rest while traveling. My first time flying on an airplane I did not sleep well the night before, it

15. Steinborn and Huestegge, "Walk Down the Lane Gives Wings to Your Brain," 795.

16. Gupta, *Keep Sharp*, ch. 1, loc 253–66 of 642.

17. Strong, *Reclaim Your Brain*, ch. 1, loc. 331 of 3889.

18. Miller, "Optimizing Brain Health," 3.

was mostly nerves and excitement, but over the course of a long night and into a very full day I soon felt the consequences of little sleep. Between changing planes, to riding on a bus to our destination, to jumping right into the events of the day I experienced a whole new level of tired. That night, as one of the people in charge shared with the group, I could not tell you what they talked about. I distinctly remember trying my hardest to focus and stay awake to no avail. The struggle was real. I kept startling myself awake, as I was sitting in a chair, and every time my head started falling, I would wake myself up. It was less than optimal. Thankfully, a short while later our leaders ended the evening and sent us on our way. Sleep came particularly fast that night, and I was able to recover quickly. Though I was more intentional about resting when I was supposed to be resting from that point on. I learned the hard way that it was nearly impossible to be fully present and focused when I was utterly exhausted and in dire need of sleep.

Healthy Habits of Rest and Relaxation

There are multiple ways to incorporate rest and relaxation into our daily lives. Newberg and Waldman argue that relaxation is key to dealing with stress, "And one of the keys to reducing stress involves conscious focusing on the breath. However, when it comes to relaxation, a dozen deep breaths are not as effective as you might think. There's a much faster way to simultaneously relax *and* raise consciousness . . . Yawn . . . But yawning doesn't just relax you—it quickly brings you into a heightened state of cognitive awareness."[19] The authors also argue,

> Yawning will relax you and bring you into a state of alertness faster than any other meditation technique I know of, and because it is neurologically contagious, it's particularly easy to teach in a group setting . . . Yawning as a mechanism for alertness, begins within the first twenty weeks after conception. It helps regulate the circadian rhythms of newborns, and this adds to the evidence that

19. Newberg and Waldman, *How GOD Changes Your Brain*, 155–57.

yawning is involved in the regulation of wakefulness and sleep. Since circadian rhythms become asynchronous when a person's normal sleep cycle is disturbed, yawing should help the late–night partygoer reset the brain's internal clock. Yawning may also ward off the effects of jet lag and ease the discomfort caused by high altitudes.[20]

Yawning has been identified as a natural way to relax and engage the brain. And I don't know about you, but even as I was writing this and thinking about it, I found myself yawning more than usual. It is catching, but in a good way and it has wonderful benefits for the mind.

Carter and Carter suggest that hydration is also critical to adequate rest. "Essentially, hydration and the function of our brain go hand in hand. A larger, hydrated brain means increased blood flow, more oxygen, and nutrient availability, allowing for increased levels of concentration, improved mood, and better sleep."[21] Proper hydration helps with focus and rest. Gupta suggests that "Sleeping well is one of the easiest and most effective ways to improve all of your brain functions, as well as your ability to learn and remember new knowledge (it improves every system in the body)."[22] There is no substitute for a decent night's sleep; a healthy habit to incorporate would be to make getting a whole night's rest a priority. When going to sleep, Dr. Leaf suggests, "Do not go to sleep worrying about your circumstances; this can upset your sleep cycle, digestion, and weight. Hand all your issues over to God—even if unsolved—and fall asleep quoting a Scripture or thinking of all the good things that have happened to you or anything that makes you happy and feel at peace."[23] Focus on blessings, not worries. 1 Peter extols the reader to give God what troubles them, "Give all your worries and cares to God, for he cares about you."[24] All means all, each person has the incredible opportunity to let go of

20. Newberg and Waldman, *How GOD Changes Your Brain*, 157.
21. Carter and Carter, *Morning Mind*, ch. 5, loc. 1123–1135 of 4183.
22. Gupta, *Keep Sharp*, ch. 1, loc. 353–62 of 642.
23. Leaf, *Think & Eat Yourself Smart*, 232.
24. 1 Pet 5:7 (NLT).

all the things that cause them worry, to accept peace in place of it, and can find genuine rest for their souls in God, and in turn, help to develop a sound mind.

5

Now What?

For God has not given us a spirit of fear, but of
power and of love and of a sound mind.

—2 TIMOTHY 1:7

ARMED WITH THE INFORMATION gleaned so far, the question for
each person becomes "what should be done with the knowledge
gained." Dr. Leaf argues that "How you understand and use your
mind is predictive of how successful you will be."[1] It will take intentionality and action to move forward well. The following steps
should be considered.

First, acknowledge there is a battle going on for the mind.
In his book *Winning the War in Your Mind*, Craig Groeschel argues, "You cannot change what you do not confront. If you ignore
the battle, you lose the battle. The apostle Paul made this truth
clear: 'We are not fighting against flesh-and-blood enemies, but
against evil rulers and authorities of the unseen world, against
mighty powers in this dark world, and against evil spirits in the

1. Leaf, *Think, Learn, Succeed*, Prologue, loc. 245 of 5409.

heavenly places' (Eph 6:12 NLT)."[2] Once one confronts the battle and the multiple components that work against one, one can win the battles that arise more efficiently.

Second, realize that God has equipped each of his children to wage war in the battle of the mind successfully and win. 2 Corinthians 10 reminds the reader, "For though we live in the world, we do not wage war as the world does. The weapons we fight with are not the weapons of the world. On the contrary, they have divine power to demolish strongholds. We demolish arguments and every pretension that sets itself up against the knowledge of God, and we take captive every thought to make it obedient to Christ."[3] God's people have been equipped to fight the battles they face.

Finally, when one knows to do better, one is compelled to do better. *The Westminster Catechism* notes two specific goals for each person to help them do better, "Man's chief end is to glorify God, and to enjoy him forever."[4] The information gained on what a sound mind is, how to improve and activate it, and healthy habits to incorporate to strengthen the mind should be continually applied. Both for one's benefit, and most importantly, so each person can honor and glorify God to the best of one's ability. Dr. Leaf argues, "For now, rest in the assurance that what God has empowered you to do with your mind is more powerful and effective than any medication, any threat, any sickness, or any neurological challenge. The Scripture is clear on this: You do not have a spirit of fear but of love, power, and a sound mind (2 Tim. 1:7)."[5] With a sound mind, one can live empowered.

While observing Dan Wegner's studies, Jonathan Haidt noted that people who are asked not to think about specific things, like a white bear, or food, struggle as it is complicated to follow those instructions. Wager noted that when one ceases working to suppress

2. Groeschel, *Winning the War in Your* Mind, Intro. loc. 400 of 2829.

3. 2 Cor 10:3–5 (NIV).

4. Westminster Divines, "Westminster Shorter Catechism (1647).

5. Leaf, *Switch On Your Brain*, 33.

a thought, it comes back quickly, making it much harder to get rid of the thought. Wegner called this an "ironic process."[6]

> When controlled processing tries to influence thought ("Don't think about a white bear!"), it sets up an explicit goal. And whenever one pursues a goal, a part of the mind automatically monitors progress, so that it can order corrections or know when success has been achieved. When that goal is an action in the world (such as arriving at the airport), this feedback system works well. But when the goal is mental, it backfires. Automatic processes continually check: "Am I not thinking about a white bear?" As the act of monitoring for the absence of the thought introduces the thought, the person must try even harder to divert consciousness. Automatic and controlled processes end up working at cross purposes, firing each other up to ever greater exertions. But because controlled processes tire quickly, eventually the inexhaustible automatic processes run unopposed, conjuring up herds of white bears. Thus, the attempt to remove an unpleasant thought can guarantee it a place on your frequent-playlist of mental ruminations.[7]

When the writer of Philippians directs the reader in things that should be thought about, "Finally, brothers and sisters, whatever is true, whatever is noble, whatever is right, whatever is pure, whatever is lovely, whatever is admirable—if anything is excellent or praiseworthy—think about such things." he did not include a list to avoid, thereby not involving an automatic process that was doomed to fail due to the minds constant progress monitoring.[8] Instead, the reader is encouraged to think about things that honor God, making an achievable mental goal that allows the automatic process to help guide the mind in a healthy direction. Selk and Reed argue that if one's primary focus is on avoiding problems, one has just inadvertently made problems the main focus.[9] One

6. Haidt, *Happiness Hypothesis*, ch. 1, loc. 527 of 704.
7. Haidt, *Happiness Hypothesis*, ch. 1, loc. 527 of 704.
8. Phil 4:13 (NIV).
9. Selk and Reed, *Relentless Solution Focus*, Preface, loc. 135 of 536.

should intentionally focus more on what one should think about than what one should not. One way to improve one's thought life is to practice reconceptualizing memories as they arise. Dr Leaf notes that one can harness the ability to do this, defining it as ". . . reconceptualization of memory—that is the deliberate, intentional, mindful, and intellectual redesigning of thoughts (and thus the structure of the brain) over time."[10] Reconceptualizing can help to change negative memories into learning moments. While reconceptualizing a memory, one can observe themselves and their thinking patterns and choose to view them differently.

One can choose positivity over negativity. Leaf suggests, "We are wired to think positively with optimism. Your body and brain are finely attuned to your uniqueness and the positivity of your mind. You are essentially wired for love, right down to the genetic level; the more you improve your mental self–care habits, the more your brain and body will respond in positive ways."[11] The more one works to think and live following the Bible, the better one will be. Selk and Reed argue, "True success boils down to thought control. Those who are happiest, healthiest, and most successful choose thoughts that biologically improve their quality of life. Mental toughness is thought control—choosing the right thoughts that make you feel better and cause you to take action on what creates positive outcomes."[12] To move towards success, one must first gain control of their thoughts. The authors also note, "Mentally tough people are significantly happier, healthier, and more successful than most people . . . mental toughness is the ability to focus on solutions, especially in the face of adversity. It is the focus on solutions instead of problems that is the key to health and success."[13] We get to choose where we focus, and what gets to take up our mental thought processes. It is like we stand guard over the door to our minds and thoughts, and get to decide what is allowed in, what we focus on, and for how long. It is both a privilege and a responsibility.

10. Leaf, *Think, Learn, Succeed*, ch. 1, loc. 620–32 of 5409.

11. Leaf, *Think, Learn, Succeed*, ch. 1, loc. 572 of 5409.

12. Selk and Reed, *Relentless Solution Focus*, ch. 1, loc. 254 of 536.

13. Selk and Reed, *Relentless Solution Focus*, ch. 1, loc. 268 of 536.

Selk and Reed argue that we need to develop mental toughness, but, "Mental toughness is not supposed to be easy. It comes more easily to some than to others, but it is a discipline that everyone has to work to maintain . . . Mental toughness is about the fight. It's about knowing this game doesn't end. 'Winning' is temporary, and sometimes it means losing 'better' than you would have had you not fought."[14] The concept of perfection can be one's greatest weakness, but to make constant progress in the right direction with one's thoughts, one can "win" even when one may feel one could have done better. Dr. Leaf suggests that "Our thoughts can either limit us to what we believe we can do or free us to develop abilities well beyond our expectations or the expectations of others. When we choose a mindset that extends our abilities rather than limits them, we will experience greater intellectual satisfaction, emotional control, and mental and physical health."[15] The ability to choose is, once again, both one's right and one's responsibility. Shawn Achor, the author of *The Happiness Advantage: How a Positive Brain Fuels Success in Work and Life*, argues that optimism and happiness are critical to success. Achor states, "Thanks to this cutting–edge science, we now know that happiness is the precursor to success, not merely the result. And that happiness and optimism actually fuel performance and achievement—giving us the competitive edge that I call the Happiness Advantage."[16] Choosing to be optimistic helps to give one a distinct benefit. Achor also noted, "Because positive brains have a biological advantage over brains that are neutral or negative, this principle teaches us how to retrain our brains to capitalize on positivity and improve our productivity and performance."[17] One's brain can function at an optimal level when one capitalizes on positivity. Achor explores six principles of what he calls the happiness advantage.

> *The Fulcrum and the Lever*—How we experience the
> world, and our ability to succeed within it, constantly

14. Selk and Reed, *Relentless Solution Focus,* preface, loc. 220 of 536.

15. Leaf, *Think, Learn, Succeed,* intro, loc. 435 of 5409.

16. Achor, *The Happiness Advantage*, Intro, loc. 66 of 367.

17. Achor, *The Happiness Advantage*, part 1, loc. 252 of 367.

changes based on our mindset . . . *The Tetris Effect*—
When our brains get stuck in a pattern that focuses on
stress, negativity, and failure, we set ourselves up to fail.
This principle teaches us how to retrain our brains to
spot patterns of possibility, so we can see—and seize—
opportunity wherever we look. *Falling Up*—In the midst
of defeat, stress, and crisis, our brains map different paths
to help us cope. *The Zorro Circle* This principle teaches us
how to regain control by focusing first on small, man-
ageable goals, and then gradually expanding our circle to
achieve bigger and bigger ones. *The 20-Second Rule* . . .
This principle shows how, by making small energy ad-
justments, we can reroute the path of least resistance and
replace bad habits with good ones. *Social Investment*—In
the midst of challenges and stress, some people choose
to hunker down and retreat within themselves. But the
most successful people invest in their friends, peers,
and family members to propel themselves forward. This
principle teaches us how to invest more in one of the
greatest predictors of success and excellence—our social
support network.[18]

Practicing these six principles can help one when facing new obstacles, and old ones as well.

When studying brain health Newberg and Waldman suggest,
"Exercise, social interaction, and optimism all tie for first place
in terms of keeping your brain healthy, and meditation comes in
second."[19] There are things we can do to keep a healthy brain and a
strong mind. Darin Olien has identified five things that help build
what he calls a "SuperLife,"

> *Nutrition.* Pretty straightforward, right? It means every-
> thing we eat. The foods themselves, and also everything
> they contain, which can be a very long list. We may not
> always know everything that's on that list, but our bodies
> do. *Hydration.* The mere fact that we are mostly water
> should be enough to explain this one. *Oxygenation.* Like
> water, we know we need it, though we don't all know the

18. Achor, *Happiness Advantage*, part 1, loc. 252–62 of 367.

19. Newberg and Waldman, *How GOD Changes Your Brain*, 210.

many reasons why. *Alkalization.* This one's a bit trickier. It has to do with the balance of acidity and alkalinity of our internal environment. *Detoxification.* This includes our immune system, which has a lot to deal with, plus the process of handling all the toxins and poisons and other junk the world throws at us.[20]

These components will all aid in living a healthier life, and in turn, help to keep a strong mind. Newberg and Waldman suggest eight different things that will improve one's physical, mental, and spiritual well-being: smiling, staying intellectually active, consciously relaxing, yawning, meditating, aerobic exercise, dialoguing with others, and having faith.[21] These various components combined have been noted to have positive outcomes and can help to build a strong mind.

Healthy Habits to Incorporate Into Each Day

There are a couple more healthy habits that help to build a sound mind that I wanted to cover, starting with journaling. Journaling has also been noted to have a positive impact on the mind. According to Dr. Rob Carter and Dr. Kirti Salwe Carter, "There are many documented health benefits to writing. Incorporating just five minutes of putting pen to paper in the morning can have a hugely beneficial impact on your day—fewer visits to the doctor, reduced blood pressure, improved mood/affect, and feeling of greater psychological well-being are just a few of the documented benefits."[22] Taking time to stop and think about what one is thinking about can have a significant impact. I have noticed this throughout the day, when I stop to think about what I am thinking about I become more introspective and aware not only of my thoughts, but what started me down the path of thoughts I was now on. The process of putting pen to paper, or typing on a device as the case maybe, can produce even more clarity at times, as it

20. Olien, *SuperLife*, part 1, loc. 147–60 of 592.

21. Newberg and Waldman, *How GOD Changes Your Brain*, 149–63.

22. Carter and Carter, *Morning Mind*, ch.10, loc. 1894 of 4183.

forces me to slow down, and think about not only my thoughts, but how to express them. I have found it can have a calming effect. I like to trace my thoughts back and find the original thought that caused me to trail off at times. It is an interesting study of oneself, to write down where a line of thoughts began, and then where it led to. It can also be quite informative to look back at journals or diaries written in the past to see what one's thoughts were about life events as they transpired. I often wish I had been more descriptive of what was going on when I wrote out my thoughts. For example, I have some journals that describe my feelings at that moment, but not what caused those feelings. Some of this is attributed to the age I was when writing, and some to the emotion. I used journaling as a way of processing, and sometimes, the emotion seemed all encompassing, so at that moment, it was the only thing on my mind. But usually, the emotion would pass as I processed through it. It can be helpful to write about one's thoughts at any point of the day, whether morning, noon, or night. But the process of taking time to express one's thoughts is good for the mind. The Drs. Carter are proponents of starting the morning with creative writing. Especially with goals in mind.

> Neuropsychologist Jenni Ogden posits the benefits of expressing oneself creatively in writing, suggesting that writing and reading something someone enjoys can slow down the brain's aging process. Another great way to start your day with writing is setting goals, as we have seen with creating more self-discipline and forming empowering habits. One study found that people who write about reaching their future goals on a regular basis are happier and have reduced stress levels. Another form of early morning writing is journaling, expressing how you feel about certain issues. Another study documented people willingly writing about traumatic events. It showed that six months after they started writing, people experienced emotional benefits because describing the trauma made them better equipped to deal with it, even if they did not talk to anyone about it.[23]

23. Carter and Carter, *Morning Mind*, ch.10, loc. 1894 of 4183.

Writing can help us process what we are going through and can help us to understand our thoughts better along the way.

If you need some inspiration to get writing the authors of *The Morning Mind* have some suggestions.

1. Write about an event that impacted you deeply.

2. Write a detailed account of someone you know.

3. Describe in detail an object in front of you.

4. Write about your perfect morning.

5. Write about a piece of music.

6. The magic wand, this is envisioning a solution to a problem.

7. Analyze the works of writers you admire.[24]

Another thing you can journal is your prayers. Craige Groeschel says this about one's prayers: "You might talk your prayers, yell your prayers, sing or journal them. You might pray long or you might pray short; just make sure you pray. There is no perfect way. Just pray."[25] This is similar to journaling, it does not have to be perfect to be an effective way to help you process and build a strong mind.

Another key element to building a strong mind is forgiveness. "Forgiveness improves family relationships, decreases depressive symptoms while enhancing empathy and life satisfaction, and it can heal a wounded romantic heart. Even the act of choosing to replace an unforgiving attitude with a forgiving one affects the peripheral and central nervous systems in ways that promote physical and psychological health."[26] There are so many benefits to forgiveness. Colossians reminds us, "Therefore, as God's chosen people, holy and dearly loved, clothe yourselves with compassion, kindness, humility, gentleness and patience. Bear with each other and forgive one another if any of you has a grievance against someone. Forgive as the Lord forgave you. And over all these virtues put

24. Carter and Carter, *Morning Mind*, ch.10, loc. 1907–1931 of 4183.

25. Groeschel, *Winning the War in Your* Mind, ch.11, loc. 2063 of 2829.

26. Newberg and Waldman, *How GOD Changes Your Brain*, 206–7.

on love, which binds them all together in perfect unity."[27] Forgiveness requires intentionality and determination. And sometimes, it requires us to continue to choose to offer forgiveness more than once. I have found that I must be careful of spending too much time dwelling or meditating on past offenses, and instead I need to be quick to forgive, even if that person never said sorry. There is so much freedom in offering forgiveness even when the person never acknowledges their offense. Sometimes, the person who offended me does not even know that they did. So, of course they are not going to apologize, they don't even realize there was hurt caused. When I can choose to forgive them, I get to walk in a freedom that brings so much peace it is always worth it. Dr. Leaf expounds on the benefits of forgiveness as well.

> We're often told to "forgive and forget" the wrongs that we suffer, but it turns out that there is scientific truth (and gut logic) behind the common saying. Research shows that the details of a transgression are more susceptible to being forgotten when that transgression has been forgiven. Adopting a forgiveness mindset is a choice, an act of your free will. It comes with extreme health benefits. Forgiveness enables you to release toxic thoughts of anger, resentment, bitterness, shame, grief, regret, guilt, and hate. It disentangles you from the source of the issue, removing the negative energy from toxic thinking. The emotions attached to the toxic thought can hold your mind in a nasty, vise-like grip. As long as these unhealthy toxic thoughts dominate your mind, you will not be able to reconceptualize your memories—that is, grow new, healthy thoughts. Scientific research shows that forgiveness and love are good for your mind, brain, and body health! Ongoing results of the "Forgiveness Study" carried out by researchers at the University of Wisconsin found that people who develop an ability to forgive have greater control over their emotions; are significantly less angry, upset, and hurt; and are much healthier. It's easier

27. Col 3:12–14 (NIV).

to move forward into a purposeful future when you have truly forgiven.[28]

Forgiveness is necessary and crucial to developing a sound mind. When I am experiencing unforgiveness I have found it helpful to think about why I am feeling what I am feeling, and journaling can help with that. Sometimes all I really want is someone to come alongside of me and acknowledge that what I am going through in that moment really stinks. In those moments what I am looking for is validation, for someone to acknowledge the hurt I am feeling and that it matters to someone. The amazing news is that everything we are go through matters to God. In Luke we can see how the details of our lives are not missed and that we matter to God. "Are not five sparrows sold for two pennies? Yet not one of them is forgotten by God. Indeed, the very hairs of your head are all numbered. Don't be afraid; you are worth more than many sparrows."[29] In moments when I want to know if my hurt matters to someone, I have found taking that question to God in prayer to be very helpful, because everything we go through matters to him. And when I know my hurt matters to God, I find it much easier to forgive the person who caused the offense.

Another element to developing a healthy mind is smiling, "Even if you don't feel like it, the mere act of smiling repetitively helps to interrupt mood disorders and strengthen the brain's neural ability to maintain a positive outlook on life."[30] So as cheesy as the saying goes to "turn that frown upside down," it really does make a difference. I enjoy smiling as a rule, yet not everything I encounter makes me want to smile, and that's ok. This is not a recommendation to be fake, but instead to choose to smile simply because you can. Dr. Leaf argues that we get to choose a happiness mindset.

> Be proactive in where you put your energy: you can choose to either bemoan and marinate in your misery or move your energy to do something constructive. It may

28. Leaf, *Think, Learn, Succeed*, ch. 6, loc. 1020–1027 of 5409.

29. Luke 12:6–7 (NIV).

30. Newberg and Waldman, *How GOD Changes Your Brain*, 151.

be as simple as smiling at someone or taking your dog for a walk. Don't allow yourself to think that I will be so happy when this is over. Enjoy the start, the middle, and the end! Tell yourself it's okay to experience different emotions, moving toward peaceful acceptance. You don't have to paint your face like a clown and pretend. You have to just be you, recognizing happiness is part of our wired-for-love design.[31]

Smiling is good for us, and has a positive impact on our minds. Smiling is such a neat thing, and it needs no translation. A smile has the power to help set people at ease and can help to make an awkward situation a little less awkward. Psalm 106 gives us a great reason to smile. "Praise the Lord. Give thanks to the Lord, for he is good; his love endures forever."[32] I have found if I am having an off–day, I like to meditate on scriptures, such as this one, and it has a way of making me smile. The fact that smiling is also good for the brain makes me want to smile just thinking about it.

This flows right into another element that is great for the mind, thankfulness and gratefulness. Smiling and thankfulness often go hand–in–hand. It is hard to imagine a person talking about what they are thankful or grateful for without a single smile. Though sometimes it can be hard to find something we are thankful for. Craig Groeschel argues we can reframe our thoughts, "We find what we are looking for, and we reframe by looking for God's goodness. I decided I would look for his goodness and be grateful. of course, the change wasn't immediate. but over time the reframe worked! searching for God's goodness transformed my attitude."[33] When we intentionally take our thoughts captive and choose to reframe how we see something by looking for God's goodness in that moment, it can have a notable impact on our lives. Drs. Carter and Carter recommend when you first wake up a few healthy habits to help you with your day. "Drink a glass of warm water with lemon. Make your bed. Say ten things for which you are grateful.

---

31. Leaf, *Think, Learn, Succeed*, ch. 7, loc. 1128 of 5409.

32. Ps 106:1 (NIV).

33. Groeschel, *Winning the War in Your* Mind, ch.9, loc. 1690 of 2829.

Simply put a smile on your face"[34] Being thankful and grateful is a wonderful habit to incorporate into one's daily life. Christians have so much to be thankful for as Francis Schaeffer reminds us,

> I have found it extremely helpful that when a man has accepted Christ as his Savior, he should bow his head and say "Thank you" to the God who is there—"Thank you for the completed work." Undoubtedly men have been saved and have gone away not consciously saying "Thank you" but how wonderful it is when a man has seen himself as a sinner, and has understood his lostness, for that man to have accepted Christ as his Savior and then to have bowed his head consciously to say "Thank you" for a work that is absolute and complete. It is usually when the newly-born one thanks God that the assurance comes, that he comes to rest in certainty and in peace. It is the same in restoration. There is a continuing parallel here. If we have sinned, it is wonderful consciously to say, "Thank you for a completed work," after we have brought that specific sin under the finished work of Christ. While not absolutely necessary for restoration, the conscious giving of thanks brings assurance and peace. We say "Thank you" for work completed upon the cross, which is sufficient for a completely restored relationship.[35]

We have so much to be thankful for, no matter what comes our way. Whether one is a new believer, or has been a Christian for many years, we will always have something to be thankful for. Dr. Leaf expounds on the benefits of being grateful.

> When we choose to be grateful, we tap into our natural design. Research on the effects gratitude has on our biology shows how being thankful increases our longevity, our ability to use our imagination, and our ability to problem-solve. It also improves our overall health. An attitude of gratitude leads to the feeling that life is worth living, which brings mental health benefits in a positive

---

34. Carter and Carter, *Morning Mind*, ch.11, loc. 2026 of 4183.

35. Schaeffer, *True Spirituality*, ch. 8, loc. 2066–2078 of 3343.

feedback loop that leads to more resilience, the ability to bounce back more quickly.[36]

When we choose to count our blessings we build a healthy habit that is excellent for the mind. I have found that when I am having a rough day, and everything seems to be going wrong, when I intentionally stop, take a couple deep breaths, and start to focus on what I am thankful for, it can change my whole outlook for the rest of the day. Sometimes that is all it takes, and sometimes I have to intentionally go back to counting my blessings. I have a mental list of things I am thankful for, and I will start going down the list: my family, my parents, siblings, nieces, and nephews, and usually at this time I will think of something one of my family members said that made me smile, or something a niece or nephew said or did that was enduring, and automatically I start to feel a little better, and the day seems to brighten just a little. Then I will keep going: my friends, my church, or a fond memory, then I will usually pause on something about one of them that made my day, and again, I smile. Then I keep going. I keep going until I realize my thoughts have been completely redirected to things that I am grateful for. And no matter the challenge, it feels a little bit more bearable. Each time I count my blessings I find it gets easier to lift my eyes off of the momentary trouble, and to seek God in that moment, effectively taking my focus off of the problem, and choosing to meditate on the goodness of God. The writer of Psalms instructs us in giving thanks. "Give thanks to the Lord, for he is good; his love endures forever."[37] The writer of Colossians also recommends thankfulness.

> Let the peace of Christ rule in your hearts, since as members of one body you were called to peace. And be thankful. Let the message of Christ dwell among you richly as you teach and admonish one another with all wisdom through psalms, hymns, and songs from the Spirit, singing to God with gratitude in your hearts. And whatever you do, whether in word or deed, do it all in the name of

36. Leaf, *Think, Learn, Succeed*, ch.10, loc. 1249 of 5409.

37. Ps 118:1 (NIV).

the Lord Jesus, giving thanks to God the Father through him.[38]

We can always give thanks, not because every circumstance is good, but because God is good, no matter the circumstance. He is seriously the best. One of my favorite sayings is, *"God's got this."* This is a good reminder that no matter what I am facing in that moment, it is not stressing God out. He has everything under control. And a great way to handle stress, is to choose thankfulness.

A great way to build gratefulness into your life is to first take stock of your thoughts. Dr. Leaf has some suggestions on this. "Gratitude begins with an awareness of whether you have an attitude of gratitude, so intentionally and critically observe your thinking to determine if an attitude of gratitude is part of it. Do you spend more time counting your blessings or more time focusing on what is missing from your life? Are you thankful? Spend the next week analyzing how grateful you are."[39] If you take the time to record your thoughts you may surprise yourself. Writing down what we are thankful for helps to engage our minds in multiple ways. To write one must focus, and spend time not only thinking about one's blessings, but how to record those blessings. It is an excellent exercise for the mind, and also something that one could journal each morning. And, I am guessing, if you are journaling about what you are thankful for, you are probably going to smile about it as well. Thankfulness is just so good for helping to develop a sound mind.

38. Col 3:15–17 (NIV).
39. Leaf, *Think, Learn, Succeed*, ch.10, loc. 1267 of 5409.

Conclusion

Since, then, you have been raised with Christ,
set your hearts on things above, where Christ is,
seated at the right hand of God. Set your minds
on things above, not on earthly things.

—COLOSSIANS 3:1–2

THOUGHTS ARE AT THE root of everything; everything starts with
a thought. Thoughts matter. Schaeffer argued that "true spirituality in the Christian life rests: in the realm of my thought–life."[1]
Thoughts are immeasurably essential and have a direct impact
on one's spiritual life. Nanez suggested that one should work
on loving God with body, spirit, and mind.[2] One should focus
on building a sound mind by involving every part of one's life
in honoring God and bringing every thought into obedience to
Christ and under his authority.[3] The definition of a sound mind as
explored in this book is a mind that has an in–depth knowledge
of Scripture, making a conscious effort to understand one's own
emotions, and working to establish habits and patterns to enhance

1. Schaeffer, *True Spirituality*, ch. 9, loc. 2333 of 3343.
2. Nañez, *Full Gospel Fractured Minds?*, 87.
3. 1 Cor 15: 27–28 (NLT).

one's mental health, including various things that keep the brain healthy. Understanding that love, power, and a sound mind work together as gifts from God and the spirit of fear is directly opposed to these. This book worked to understand the purpose of good neurotheology and encourage a better understanding of healthy practices and habits to develop a sound mind.

One needs a sound mind to live a life that honors God and does not give in to sin. Schaeffer suggests that moral battles are first won or lost in the mind.[4] One should not ignore the battle going on for the mind, but one should actively engage in it with the weapons God has given each of his people. "For though we live in the world, we do not wage war as the world does. The weapons we fight with are not the weapons of the world. On the contrary, they have divine power to demolish strongholds. We demolish arguments and every pretension that sets itself up against the knowledge of God, and we take captive every thought to make it obedient to Christ."[5] To build a sound mind, one must be actively involved in the process. This book looked at four specific components that impact the ability to develop a sound mind. Focus, is the ability to take one's thoughts captive and work towards a specific goal. Meditation, the health and spiritual benefits that come from it, and the multiple perspectives on it. Diet and Exercise and how what one consumes directly impact one's ability to think and process. Furthermore, the last component of building a sound mind that this book delved into was rest and relaxation and the necessity to get adequate rest and downtime to help the mind operate efficiently. Finally, this book explored what all this information combined means and how one should respond as well some more healthy habits to incorporate into each day.

Focus requires one to choose what one is thinking. Daniel Goleman defined it as taking possession with the mind over one thing out of multiple simultaneous options.[6] Focus requires intentionality. The writer of Proverbs urges the reader with verbs such

4. Schaeffer, *True Spirituality*, ch. 9, loc. 2182 of 3343.

5. 2 Cor 10:3–5 (NIV).

6. Goleman, *Focus: The Hidden Driver of Excellence*, ch.1, loc. 219 of 5627.

as turn, apply, call, cry, look, and search, showing that attention requires action.[7] The questions to be considered are, are the things thought about worth giving oneself to, worth growing, and worth resembling? If one is trying to live a life pleasing to God, one needs to focus on things that honor God and continually repeat this process. Building a sound mind requires not just rejecting and turning from what is not excellent, but actively focusing on God and worshiping him, immersing oneself fully in delighting in the Lord, "Set your minds on things that are above, not on things that are on earth."[8] The Bible gives clear directions on where one should focus their thoughts.[9]

Meditation can be both internal in focusing the mind and external in participating in activities like journaling, singing, and chanting. Finley argued that everything one participates in can become a form of meditation on God and awareness of his presence.[10] A deeper awareness of God is the goal of meditation, and the process is good for the brain in building a strong mind. There are multiple benefits to meditating on the word of God. While meditation is understood to help the brain, the debate continues about what kind of meditation. There are many ways to meditate, and contemplating spiritual things, in particular, has a profound impact. John Main suggests that Christian meditation has the goal of becoming aware of God in everything. "The all –important aim in Christian meditation is to allow God's mysterious and silent presence within us to become more and more not only *a* reality, but *the* reality in our lives; to let it become that reality which gives meaning, shape and purpose to everything we do, to everything we are."[11] Christian meditation aims to become aware of the presence of God in everything one does.

Understanding how meditation helps to build a sound mind, there are multiple habits one can incorporate into their life to reap

7. Prov 2:1–5 (NIV).
8. Col 3:2 (NIV).
9. Phil 4:8 (NIV).
10. Finley, *Christian Meditation*, 4.
11. John Main, *Word into Silence*, 4.

the benefits of meditation. Leaf recommends prayer as well for meditation. "When we pray, when we catch our thoughts, when we memorize and quote scripture, we move into this deep meditative state."[12] One should intentionally focus on things that honor God while actively directing one's thoughts to the word of God. When one meditates on something specific, they are directing their mind not only on what to focus on but also on what to avoid. Clowney argues there are three dimensions of Christian meditation, the first is it is grounded in the truth of God, second, it responds to the love of God, and third, these lead the Christian to worship God.[13] There is a progression for one while meditating on the truth of God. Newberg and Waldman argue that exercise can be viewed as a form of meditation as it involves continuous concentration and a conscious regulation of breathing and movements.[14] Meditation and exercising both improve the brain and help to build a sound mind.

Diet and exercise are uniquely crucial to building a sound mind as what one consumes will directly fuel the brain's ability to be healthy. Leaf argues, "How and what we eat affects our mind, brain, and body."[15] The impact on the brain is one reason to be conscientious of what one is eating. All the components, one's spirit, soul, and body, were designed to work together, and they are at their best when they do. The benefits of exercise impact the mind in multiple ways. Newberg and Waldman argue that "vigorous exercise strengthens every part of the brain, as well as what it is connected to–the body."[16] 1 Timothy 4 reminds the reader, "For physical training is of some value, but godliness has value for all things, holding promise for both the present life and the life to come."[17] Exercise and physical training have value and should not be discarded. Romans 12 exhorts us, "Therefore, I urge you, brothers and sisters, in view of God's mercy, to offer your bodies as

12. Leaf, *Switch On Your Brain*, 84.

13. Clowney, *Christian Meditation*, 9.

14. Newberg and Waldman, *How GOD Changes Your Brain*, 160.

15. Leaf, *Think & Eat Yourself Smart*, 84–85.

16. Newberg and Waldman, *How GOD Changes Your Brain*, 160–61.

17. 1 Tim 4:8 (NIV)

a living sacrifice, holy and pleasing to God—this is your true and proper worship. Do not conform to the pattern of this world, but be transformed by the renewing of your mind. Then you will be able to test and approve what God's will is—his good, pleasing and perfect will."[18] From these verses, the readers are reminded of essential components of true and proper worship and that once one's mind is renewed, it is renewed for a purpose, to understand God's will. Everything one does in building a sound mind should revolve around knowing that one should understand what God's will is and then determine to live out his will to the best of one's ability. Healthy habits to incorporate would be to integrate a healthy diet and exercise into one's life daily. What kind of diet and exercises are up to the individual. There are a plethora of sources to guide each individual to find the best dietary plan for them, and it all begins with a choice and intentionality. Moreover, about exercise, Strong argues that an inactive lifestyle that forgoes exercise will have adverse outcomes for overall health. The good news is the result of being reasonably active can have a positive effect.[19] There are a great many benefits of a healthy diet and exercise on the brain, and in turn, it helps to build a strong mind. We need to keep a healthy balance and understand that eating mindfully and exercising are valuable, and getting rest is essential to improve all of the habits previously mentioned.

Rest and relaxation are also essential components of building a sound mind. Leaf suggests, "Sleep is needed to regenerate and protect the proper biological function of both our bodies and minds and to consolidate memory."[20] Our bodies need rest; how much varies from person to person, but rest is vital. Multiple Psalms speak about our need for rest and emphasize that real rest is found only in God.[21] Relaxation should be an intentional part of one's day as it is essential. Gupta advocates that "Our everyday experiences, including what we eat, how much we exercise, with

---

18. Rom 12:1–2 (NIV).

19. Strong, *Reclaim Your Brain*, ch. 1, loc. 341 of 3889.

20. Leaf, *Think & Eat Yourself Smart*, 206.

21. Ps 62:1 (NIV).

whom we socialize, what challenges we face, how well we sleep, and what we do to reduce stress and learn, factor much more into our brain health and overall wellness than we can imagine."[22] Rest is a key to keeping a healthy mind. Healthy habits of rest and relaxation to incorporate are focused breathing, intentional yawning, and proper hydration. Leaf suggests not going to sleep worrying but instead falling asleep quoting Scripture and counting one's blessings.[23] Isaiah reminds his readers how to find rest and peace, "You will keep in perfect peace those whose minds are steadfast, because they trust in you."[24] Rest and relaxation are necessary for building and maintaining a sound mind.

There is a battle going on for the mind, and God has equipped his people to fight in this battle successfully. When one learns new information to help them live better, they are compelled to do so. When learning new information on developing a good theology of a sound mind, it is recommended that it be practiced for the ultimate goal of bringing glory to God to understand his will better and live in accordance with it. Real success will come down to thought control, as successful people direct their thoughts.[25] As one develops better thought control, one will also develop mental toughness. A few more healthy habits that one can incorporate into their daily life to help build a strong mind are: journaling, forgiveness, smiling, and thankfulness. A good neurotheology should involve knowledge of the brain, how it works and what habits to include to improve the brain's functioning. Also, examining how to build a sound mind by intentionally taking control of one's thoughts to make them obedient to Christ. This can be done by replacing what one currently thinks about with God's truth and his word with the express purpose of glorifying God with every part of one's life and not giving into sin. Starting at the beginning, where everything starts, with a thought in the mind.

22. Gupta, *Keep Sharp*, ch.1, loc. 253–66 of 642.

23. Leaf, *Think & Eat Yourself Smart*, 232.

24. Isa 26:3 (NIV).

25. Selk and Reed, *Relentless Solution Focus*, intro. loc. 254 of 536.

Bibliography

Achor, Shawn. *The Happiness Advantage: How a Positive Brain Fuels Success in Work and Life*. New York: Crown, 2010. Kindle.

Carter, Robert, III, and Kirti Salwe Carter. *The Morning Mind: Use Your Brain to Master Your Day and Supercharge Your Life*. USA: HarperCollins Leadership, 2019. Kindle.

Chérif, Lobna, et al. "Multitasking in the Military: Cognitive Consequences and Potential Solutions." *Applied Cognitive Psychology* 32 (2018) 429–39.

Clowney, Edmund P. *Christian Meditation: What the Bible teaches about meditation and spiritual exercises*. Vancouver: Regent College Publishing, 1979.

Dance, Jeffery W., and Robert W. Service. "The Attractive Nuisance: A Model to Prevent Workplace Distractions." *Journal of Multidisciplinary Research (1947–2900)* 5 (2013) 35–51.

Doehring, Carrie. "Minding the Gap When Cognitive Neuroscience Is a Cognate Discipline in Pastoral Theology: Lessons from Neurotheology." *Journal of Pastoral Theology* 20 (2010) 93–108.

Fikkert, Brian, and Kelly M. Kapic. *Becoming Whole: Why the Opposite Of Poverty Isn't The American Dream*. Chicago, IL: Moody, 2019.

Finley, James. *Christian Meditation: Experiencing the PRESENCE OF GOD*. San Francisco: HarperCollins, 2004.

Goleman, Daniel. *Focus: The Hidden Driver of Excellence*. New York: HarperCollins, 2013. Kindle.

Groeschel, Craig. *Winning the War in Your Mind*. Grand Rapids, MI: Zondervan, 2021. Kindle.

Gupta, Sanjay MD. *Keep Sharp: Build a Better Brain at Any Age*. New York: Simon & Schuster, 2021. Kindle.

Haidt, Jonathan. *The Happiness Hypothesis: Finding Modern Truths in Ancient Wisdom*. New York: Basic, 2006. Kindle.

Hansen, Anders. *The Real Happy Pill: Power Up Your Brain by Moving Your Body*. New York: Skyhorse, 2016. Kindle.

Bibliography

Hirschlag, Allison. "Naps Don't Work for Everyone. Genetic Differences Are Why." *The Washington Post*, March 7, 2020. https://www.washingtonpost.com/health/naps-dont-work-for-everyone-genetic-differences-are-why/2020/03/06/fd3298aa-5a73-11ea-9000-f3cffee23036_story.html.

Hodder, Alan D. *Thoreau's Ecstatic Witness*. New Haven & London: Yale University Press, 1993.

Hunter, George G., III. *The Celtic Way Of Evangelism: How Christianity Can Reach the West . . . AGAIN*. Nashville: Abingdon, 2010.

Kaczmarek, Lukasz, and Jolanta Enko, Małgorzata Awdziejczyk, Natalia Hoffmann, Natalia Białobrzeska, Przemysław Mielniczuk, and Stephan Dombrowski. "Would You Be Happier If You Looked Better? A Focusing Illusion." *Journal of Happiness Studies* 17 (2016) 357–65.

Kalas, J. Ellsworth. *Preaching in an Age of Distraction*. Downers Grove, IL: InterVarsity, 2014. Kindle.

Leaf, Caroline. *Switch On Your Brain: The Key to Peak Happiness, Thinking, and Health*. Grand Rapids, MI: Baker, 2013.

———. *Think & Eat Yourself Smart*. Grand Rapids, MI: Baker, 2016.

———. *Think, Learn, Succeed: Understanding And Using Your Mind To Thrive At School, The Workplace, And Life*. Grand Rapids, MI: Baker, 2018. Kindle.

Main, John. *Word into Silence*. Norwich: Canterbury, 2006.

Mantua, Janna, and Rebecca M. C. Spencer. "Exploring the Nap Paradox: Are Mid–Day Sleep Bouts a Friend or Foe?" *Sleep Medicine* 37 (September 17, 2017) 88–97.

Miller, John J. "Optimizing Brain Health." *Psychiatric Times* 36 (2019) 3–26.

Milner, Catherine E., and Kimberly A. Cote. "Benefits of Napping in Healthy Adults: Impact of Nap Length, Time of Day, Age, and Experience with Napping." *Journal of Sleep Research* 18 (2009) 272–81.

Mosconi, Lisa, Ph.D. *Brain Food: The Surprising Science of Eating for Cognitive Power*. New York: Penguin, 2018. Kindle.

Nañaz, Rick M. *Full Gospel Fractured Minds?* Grand Rapids, MI: Zondervan, 2005.

Newberg, Andrew M.D. and Mark Robert Waldman. *How GOD Changes Your Brain*. New York: Ballantine, 2009.

Olien, Darin. *SuperLife: The 5 Simple Fixes That Will Make You Healthy, Fit, And Eternally Awesome*. New York: Harper Wave, 2015. Kindle.

Otis, Pauletta. "Responding to Religious Violence: Love, Power, and a Sound Mind." *Brandywine Review of Faith & International Affairs* 2 (2004) 37–41.

Parker, J.Z. *Bible Diet, An Apple A Day*. New York: NYBookz, 2015.

Perlmutter, David, and Kristin Loberg. *Brain Maker: The Power of Gut Microbes to Heal and Protect Your Brain for Life*. New York: Little, Brown and Company, 2015. Kindle.

Pincott, Jena. "WICKED THOUGHTS." *Psychology Today* 48 (2015) 52–89.

Robinson, William. "How to Keep a Sound Mind." *The Journal of Pastoral Care* 6 (1952) 55.

Schaeffer, Francis. *True Spirituality*. Wheaton, IL: Tyndale, 1971. Kindle.

Bibliography

Selk, Jason, and Ellen Reed. *Relentless Solution Focus: Train Your Mind to Conquer Stress, Pressure, and Underperformance*. New York: McGraw–Hill Education, 2021. Kindle.

Simmons, Daniel. "'We Shall Be like Him, for We Shall See Him': Augustine's De Trinitate and the Purification of the Mind." *International Journal of Systematic Theology* 15 (2013) 240–64.

Steinborn, Michael B. and Lynn Huestegge. "A Walk Down the Lane Gives Wings to Your Brain. Restorative Benefits of Rest Breaks on Cognition and Self–Control." *Applied Cognitive Psychology* 30 (2016) 795–805. doi:10.1002/acp.3255.

Strong, Todd. *Reclaim Your Brain: Optimize Cognitive Function, Fight Dementia, Memory Problems, Resolve Anxiety and Depression Using Natural Methods*. N.p.: Kindle, 2020. Kindle.

Tverberg, Lois. *Reading the Bible with Rabbi Jesus*. Grand Rapids, MI: Baker, 2017. Kindle.

Westminster Divines. "The Westminster Shorter Catechism (1647) by Westminster Divines." Ligonier Ministries. Accessed February 12, 2021. https://www.ligonier.org/learn/articles/westminster-shorter-catechism/.